AN ANTHOLOGY OF COMIC CANADIAN POETRY

EDITED BY DOUGLAS BARBOUR AND STEPHEN SCOBIE

THE MAPLE LAUGH FOREVER

Illustrated by DAVID SHAW.

HURTIG PUBLISHERS EDMONTON

Hurtig Publishers Ltd.
10560-105 Street
Edmonton, Alberta

Canadian Cataloguing in Publication Data

Main entry under title:
The Maple laugh forever

Includes index.
ISBN 0-88830-198-7 (bound).
ISBN 0-88830-204-5 (pbk.)

1. Humorous poetry, Canadian.   2. Canadian
poetry (English) — 20th century.*   I. Barbour,
Douglas, 1940-   II. Scobie, Stephen, 1943-
PS8287.H8M36   C811'.0708   C81-091188-4
PR9195.85.H8M36

Associate editor: Sarah Reid
Design: David Shaw & Associates Ltd.
Printed and bound in Canada by John Deyell Company

Contents

Prologue

our forefathers literary
had little laugh or quippery
even Can. Lit. profs are still uncertain
of Haliburton
& all their students reassembling
Carman's skeleton
never found the funny bone
(beware the jokes of Archibald Lampman
they'll give you cramp, man)
Grove was grave & Mair still more
& though they made a Baron out of Gilbert Parker
his prose just went on getting darker
Sir Charles G.D. Roberts couldn't see
in all his g.d. woods   Silenus in a tree
— well yes there was our northern loon our Leacock
subtle as a duck   & laughing like a peacock

Earle Birney
from "Them Able Leave Her Ever"

Earle Birney's humorous poem reflects the widespread assumption — indeed, almost the cliché — that Canadian poetry lacks humour. Our literature is commonly perceived as dour, grim, and Northern; our images, so we are told, are of "survival" in a "harsh and lovely land." Our stories are of failures and victims, our heroes freeze in snowdrifts, and our marriages — like most of our shipping — end up on the rocks.

This anthology is dedicated to disturbing, or at least to modifying, that gloomy view. But we have to admit at the outset that Birney's image of "our forefathers literary," although incomplete, does have a good deal of evidence to support it. In making our selections, we had to recognise that there were several major poets who would have to be excluded. We became the despair of our friends, who witnessed us reading through some of Canada's finest books and dismissing them with the phrase, "No funny poems." Sometimes a single line would sparkle with an (often acerbic) wit, but we were after poems whose principal intent was to make their readers laugh. And of these there were often few enough.

There are many possible reasons for this scarcity of humour, from the fragility of the national psyche to the meteorological environment. Our national gesture is the grimace in the teeth of a blizzard, not the warm-hearted guffaw on a Mediterranean shore. One of the more literary reasons is that the roots of our poetry are in the nineteenth century, in a period which was colonial and Romantic, and neither of these attributes are conducive to humour.

A poet who takes himself solemnly (which isn't quite the same thing as taking himself seriously) finds it difficult to devote a whole poem to anything as trivial as a joke. One of the marks of the immature poet, or indeed of a whole literature which has not yet attained self-confidence, is the straining after big, "serious" topics. Sir Charles G. D. Roberts, in "The Poet Is Bidden to Manhattan Island," may have felt able to joke about Manhattan, but he undoubtedly saw his proper domain as being "In the wide awe and wisdom of the night" (which we exclude from this anthology on the grounds that we are interested only in *intentionally* funny poems: a consideration which also elimi-nates a lot of Bliss Carman.) The Canadian inferiority complex, which even today leads to much unprofitable anguish on the need to supply a recipe for "the Canadian identity," does not allow a poet the luxury of making a fool of himself in public.

Furthermore, when the colonial poet looked to the centre of Empire, what he saw was Romanticism; his precept was Matthew Arnold's "High Seriousness"; and his model was William Wordsworth, who can scarcely be called a laugh-a-minute comedian. Poetry for the Romantics was no laughing matter; even their social criticism was cast in the mould of polemic rather than satire.

Satire is a Classical form, and Canadian poetry has never had a very strong Classical tradition. When humour does start to make a genuine contribution to Canadian poetry, it is through the medium of satire, with F. R. Scott's "The Canadian Authors Meet," a poem as devastatingly accurate today as it was in 1927. And the somewhat tenuous tradition of Classical wit continues from Scott through George Johnston to Francis Sparshott, all of whom, as a consequence, are well represented in this anthology. But Romanticism re-mains the dominant mode of Canadian poetry, whether it be "black" (Leonard Cohen), or feminist (Margaret Atwood), or open-ended and rambunctious (Al Purdy). Canadian Romanticism has learned to be less solemn, but it is still comparatively rare to hear in Canada the full blast of a liberating, totally anarchic humour like Artie Gold's, with something to offend every taste.

From the 1920s on, humour becomes more and more visible in Canadian poetry, and the example and prestige of F. R. Scott have made no small contribution to this development. In 1957, Scott and A. J. M. Smith edited *The Blasted Pine*, an anthology of "satire, invective and disrespectful verse." Although we were at one stage tempted to call this collection *The Blasted Repine*, our aims, in fact, differ somewhat from those of the earlier volume. *The Blasted Pine* contained many poems which — though fine examples of satire — were not particularly *funny*. We have gone for the jokes at the expense of non-humorous satire; we have also, with due consideration, claimed that we are presenting "poetry" rather than "verse." We have, therefore, kept to a minimum examples of doggerel, parody, and deliberately bad poetry (though, of course, no collection of this kind could be complete without at least one poem from the Sweet Songstress of Saskatchewan, the immortal Sarah Binks).

A poem which is both funny *and* a good poem is a tricky combination, for a good joke is funniest the first time it is heard, whereas a good poem gets better each time it is reread. But we do believe that this is a balance which has been struck, frequently, by Canadian poets in recent years. The majority of the poems in our selection come from the years *since* the first edition of *The Blasted Pine*, and in that period the humorous poem has flourished in Canada in a way which must have exceeded Frank Scott's wildest hopes (and, perhaps, Charles G. D. Roberts' wildest fears).

Contemporary Canadian poets certainly seem more willing to make fools of themselves; we have lost that conception of the poet as a sacrosanct and hieratic figure, brooding palely on the metaphysical mysteries. Poets like Layton, Birney, and Purdy did a good deal to demystify the poet's public image, though the media distortions of Margaret Atwood and Susan Musgrave show hankerings after the old icons. The greater availability of publishing outlets in the sixties and early seventies (a situation which is at present under some threat) relieved the pressure on poets to explain the universe every time out of the gate. And the tremendous popularity of public poetry readings in recent years, thanks to the Canada Council and the League of Canadian Poets, has made its contribution — for everyone who has ever had to jolly an audience along through the heavy stuff knows the value of throwing in a few good jokes to keep the listeners awake.

This anthology contains all styles of humour, from the belly laugh to the quiet smile, from political satire to absurd anecdote, from affectionate ribaldry to black comedy. Our contention is that the humorous mode may well be the vehicle for poetry as serious, as intelligent, as beautiful, and as profound as poetry written in other, more "respectable" modes. For instance, a piece like P. K. Page's "Stefan" presents an acute and even disturbing insight into the nature of thought and language, an insight which is not in the least diminished, but rather intensified, by the humorous twist of its ending. Or Robert Allen's "Aftermath of a Planewreck: Tenerife," which many readers may not find "funny" at all, uses humour as a method of making the unthinkable, for a moment, grotesquely real. Poems like these — and there are many in the book — demonstrate the capacity of Canadian poets to use comedy for entirely serious poetic purposes.

It would be too much to say that the image of Canadian literature as obsessed with gloom and doom is a completely false one. Obviously, most of our poetry is intensely serious, and no honest attempt to deal with the nature of the human condition in the late twentieth century can escape the grim realities. But the evidence of this anthology will show, we hope, that there is another aspect of our national literary character, and that, increasingly, our writers have been able to embody a comic vision of life in poems that can hold their own, as poems, with any others being written in Canada today.

Stephen Scobie
Douglas Barbour

University of Alberta
January 1981

Oh Canada, Eh?

Negotiating a New Canadian Constitution
Lionel Kearns

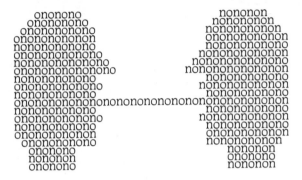

Canadiana
Daniel G. Ray

woke up this morning
a beaver in my mouth
tail wedged up under my brain
a steady beating against
the back of eyeballs
(he must have been excited)
and when i opened my mouth
a furry scream for wood.

A Sovereign Nation
Joe Wallace

Ours is a sovereign nation
Bows to no foreign will
But whenever they cough in Washington
They spit on Parliament Hill.

Canadian Poem
Raymond Fraser

There are 37 states in the United States
You see them on their flag, which has 28 stars
     to represent the original 28 German Colonies
and nine bars, coloured red and green, four green
    and five red
     to represent the territories later added
       in 1862 the year of Independence
   from France
The first Prime Minister of the United States
was Thomas Lincoln, who discovered electricity
     and made the world's first kite
He was born in the capitol of the United States
    Los Angeles, the second largest city
     in Oklahoma
The present Prime Minister of the United States
    Ronald Ali, leading socialist
    and former communist, still maintains
ties with the Party
The United States is militarily aligned
with Cuba and South Africa, an alliance she
    has unbrokenly maintained
since her defeat in the First World War
     by Canada
Military service in the U.S. is optional, all
    women from the age of 13 have the choice
    of serving in either of the two forces
or representing their families in Congress, the
    advising body to the King of the U.S.
All males are exempt from service
The most famous painter in the United States today
    is Spiro Nixon, a former bohemian
   who has now gained the respect of the
     academics, despite the avant-gardism
    of his works
The most famous writer is Raquel Hoffa
   who has written novels as well as
    poems

The most famous musical group is The Band
which is a group of Canadians
who couldn't make it at home
The biggest industry in the United States
        is fur trapping
The most popular sport is bear-baiting
                although fox hunting is popular with
                        the aristocracy
The population of the U.S. is fast approaching the
        fifty thousand mark
                due to an open door policy
        in immigration, most of the
immigrants being Atheists from Mainland China
        attracted by the commune-centered
                life of their new country's cities
The weather in the U.S. is stable, varying from
        10 to 11 degrees fahrenheit
                every day of the year
                        throughout the country
No movies have yet been made in the United States
        nor do they have television
They have no police either, because they have no
        need of these, being a relatively
                peaceful nation
Geographically the U.S. is situated Northeast
        of Canada, and in area
        is approximately the size of Wales
The average income of the citizens is 14 dollars
                a week
Although there are some automobiles there
        the most common form of transportation
        is the snowshoe
It is expected that Canada will shortly annex
        the United States
as soon as our water gets dirty enough
Then we will send the United Statesers back
        to communist France where they belong

Charité, Espérance et Foi
(a tender tale from early ca-nada)
Earle Birney

Once there were 3 little Indian girls
Champlain adopted them from the Montagnais
to show King Louis & the Cardinal it was possible
to make Christian Ladies out of savages
He baptized them Foi (11) Espérance (12) et Charité (15)
then put them in a fort to learn their French

Little Faith wriggled away & split for the woods
but Hope & Charity quickly mastered irregular verbs
& sewing   developed bosoms   went on to embroidery
When Champlain saw they had acquired piety & table manners
he dressed them in style & sailed downstream to Tadoussac
en route to the French Court with Espérance et Charité

But a wicked merchant named Nicholas Marsolet of Tadoussac
got Espérance aside & told her she was what he had to have
She said she had a date in France with King & God
Nick snarled he could have her & her sister given back
to the Indians   & grabbed her round her corset
She pulled a knife & got away to Charité

Les deux étudiantes then wrote Nicholas a letter
Hope began it:
   "Monsieur Marsolet, it was an honour & a pleasure to
   meet you, & I look forward to our next rencontre.
   'In anticipation I have sharpened my knife so that
   I may on that occasion give myself the added joy
   of cutting out your heart"
& Charity added:
   "It will give me, monsieur, great pleasure
   to help my sister eat it."
All this sounded more elegant in the original of course
because that was in correct seventeenth-century French

*

They showed their letter to Champlain
He was impressed   no mistakes in tenses
He told them he was proud they had stood firm
especially against that méchant marchand Marsolet
who ate meat both Fridays & Saturdays   an Anglophile
& sold hooch to their cousin Indians in Tadoussac
However   Champlain added   he didn't think
that Espérance et Charité were ready yet for France

The two young ladies wept   unrolled their broderie
Champlain agreed they were bien civilisées
They went down on their knees   showed him their petticoats
Champlain was kind   admired the sewing   but was firm
It was France   he said   that wasnt ready yet for them
He gave them each a wooden rosary
& sent them back to Québec with Guillaume Couillard

Couillard was a respectable churchwarden & crop inspector
no merchant   he couldnt read & had 10 children of his own
He was the first to use the plough in Canada

but when Champlain got back from France nobody knew
where Hope & Charity had got to
or if they ever found their Faith again

Montréal 1967

Troubles at Caraquet
Colleen Thibaudeau

The School Act of 1871 cd hardly be changed for New Brunswick.
Now we're in Caraquet and it's 1875
at a syndicate meeting where as usual the minority
elects a majority. Some of our old Acadians get riled.
As often happens there's a bit of a tumult
and the stovepipes get torn down. Everyone
lends a hand and sets it all straight again.
Going away the crowd sings and fires a few shots
in the air   it's an old custom
all public meetings are a bit of a mardigras.
They even give a send-off to the evening
by firing a few shots outside the door of
the Honorable Robert Young, President of the Executive Council,
he was quite used to it   but
unfortunately he was down in Fredericton
at the Legislature   had
he been home he'd have come out for a chat.
                Madame Young
got frightened and sent a hush-hush telegram
to her husband

                meanwhile everyone went happily
home even those who weren't drunk went home.

                The telegram
brought in the military from Chatham,
eighty miles away   they arrived within 24 hours.
Philéas Mailloux's place was a gathering suitable
for calming down the women & children
for wondering what the soldiers were doing in Caraquet.

                They come in.
Mailloux is covering the room from the attic
Soldier Gifford mounts
                        they fire together
and two men are dead in Caraquet.

Lots of prisoners are taken
marched to Bathurst in the terror of winter
and I'll list their names for you
all good Christians and respected citizens
and in my next chapter I'll tell you how we got them off,
though it was difficult
(it was a great tragedy)
but they had done nothing

believe me, it's an old custom
all public meetings are a bit of a mardigras.

W.L.M.K.

F. R. *Scott*

How shall we speak of Canada,
Mackenzie King dead?
The Mother's boy in the lonely room
With his dog, his medium and his ruins?

He blunted us.

We had no shape
Because he never took sides,
And no sides
Because he never allowed them to take shape.

He skilfully avoided what was wrong
Without saying what was right,
And never let his on the one hand
Know what his on the other hand was doing.

The height of his ambition
Was to pile a Parliamentary Committee on a Royal Commission,
To have 'conscription if necessary
But not necessarily conscription',
To let Parliament decide—
Later.

Postpone, postpone, abstain.

Only one thread was certain:
After World War I
Business as usual,
After World War II
Orderly decontrol.
Always he led us back to where we were before.

He seemed to be in the centre
Because we had no centre,
No vision
To pierce the smoke-screen of his politics.

Truly he will be remembered
Wherever men honour ingenuity,
Ambiguity, inactivity, and political longevity.

Let us raise up a temple
To the cult of mediocrity,
Do nothing by halves
Which can be done by quarters.

William Lyon Mackenzie King
Dennis Lee

William Lyon Mackenzie King
Sat in the middle & played with string
And he loved his mother like *anything* —
William Lyon Mackenzie King.

Election Song
Alden Nowlan

Down the street they came with torches
like a roaring human sea,
chanting, "Up with Sir Mackenzie Bowell!
Statesman! Man of Destiny!"

Mackenzie Bowell, Mackenzie Bowell,
may thoughts of your vanished fame
help us keep things in perspective
as we vote for what's-his-name.

National Identity

F. R. Scott

The Canadian Centenary Council
Meeting in le Reine Elizabeth
To seek those symbols
Which will explain ourselves to ourselves
Evoke bi-cultural responses
And prove that something called Canada
Really exists in the hearts of all
Handed out to every delegate
At the start of proceedings
A portfolio of documents
On the cover of which appeared
In gold letters
        not
A Mari Usque Ad Mare
        not
Dieu Et Mon Droit
        not
Je Me Souviens
        not
E Pluribus Unum
        but
COURTESY OF COCA-COLA LIMITED

1963

Bonne Entente

F. R. Scott

The advantages of living with two cultures
Strike one at every turn,
Especially when one finds a notice in an office building:
"This elevator will not run on Ascension Day";
Or reads in the *Montreal Star:*
"Tomorrow being the Feast of the Immaculate Conception,
There will be no collection of garbage in the city";
Or sees on the restaurant menu the bilingual dish:

DEEP APPLE PIE

TARTE AUX POMMES PROFONDES

Fuel Crisis
J. O. *Thompson*

Half the time I Britishly say *petrol*,
the other half Canadianly *gas*;

say both (1973) a lot
now there's less.

Were there ever to be none at all —
my dear Alberta dry too, or withholding —
left with two names for a lack, how hard I'd find it

to choose the fittingest homonym: the state
such matter's in as, for example, the air;
or the sea bird whose epithet is *stormy.*

Celebration
Fraser Sutherland

May 27, 1971

Great things are happening in this Canada of ours.
In Guelph, they're restoring John McCrae's house,
("In Flanders Fields the poppies blow")
and in Ottawa a 23-year old Carleton University
arts student and an 18-year old girl were fined $25 for
copulating on the lawn of the National Arts Centre.
What a tribute to Carleton, granter
of degrees in journalism and diplomas in public
administration, to have produced this paragon.
For who can say any longer
that Ottawa lacks night-life?
The partners' ethnic backgrounds are not given,
the newspapers' prudent practice. But what a wonderful
thing if the girl were French and the boy English.
Picture the primal celebration
of our dual cultures, in our capital,
in front of a national edifice, a kind
of miraculous symbiosis, like
Pierre Elliot Trudeau.
It's time to take off our
hats to these grand kids, young
but public-spirited.

After Joe Clark Winning the Federal Election
Sharon Thesen

The East Indian proprietor of
Jensen's Hardware
was happy about Joe Clark winning
the Federal Election.
So, we've got a new government now!
he had to say three times
because I didn't understand
his pronunciation of
government. It sounded like
guddamend & then it
sounded like gunnamann
& at first I thought it had
something to do with the extension cord
I was buying (which it does),
& finally I heard him & said Oh yes,
a new government,
& his bright brown face smiling
at the cash register
doing his business
with his brother-in-law standing
arms folded near the paint
also smiling in bright white shirt,
& what could I say without
ruining his morning, his friendly neighbourhood
merchantness,
make a sour face or not respond at all?
especially after he'd said it three times
& even after that embarrassment
hadn't failed in enthusiasm
& so I said, Yes,
let's hope it's a good one,
& I was probably also smiling
& that was fine, a good one,
to say that.

Border Skirmish
David McFadden

In a laundromat
in the east end
of Hamilton
Ontario
at 7:30
on a Sunday morning
a lovely lady named Joan
runs out of change and so
runs across the street
to the McDonald Hamburgatorium
standing now where once stood
the house where she was born.

She hands the girl a five-dollar bill
and asks for change for the laundry machines
and the girl is kind of bitchy
and says I can't give you no change,
I need all I got
as if anyone who would be out of change
on a Sunday morning
in the east end
of Hamilton
Ontario
is some kind of degenerate.

Shee-it says Joan, a billion burgers
you've sold in this once-proud land
and you can't even change a five
to help a native in a Sunday morning jam.
Okay then give me a cup of tea.

We don't have tea
says the girl
superiorly
(tea being basically
an unamerican drink)
then give me a cup of coffee says Joan
who never drinks coffee
and she hands the girl the five
and the girl looks a little sick

as if the founder of the firm
is looking over her shoulder
and has caught her with her finger
up her bum
or up somebody else's bum
but what can she do
nothing
so she hands over a coffee
and two two-dollar bills
and three quarters in change.

So Joan with a funny little smile
hands the girl back one of the twos
and says now I'd like an orange juice
and the girl thinks to herself
oh shit
but what can she do
nothing
so she hands over an orange juice
and a one-dollar bill
and three quarters in change.

So Joan with the same little smile
gives the girl the other two
and says now I'd like a Danish
and the girl's eyes go up to heaven
or what passes for heaven in McDonaldland
and her face turns bright red
and her wig starts bouncing up and down
but what could she do
nothing
so she hands over the Danish
and another one-dollar bill
and three quarters.

So now in case you haven't been counting
Joan has managed to get nine quarters
in change out of McDonald's

a small victory really
just barely worth recording in verse
because she's paid for every one
of those nine quarters

oh how she's paid.

Calgary poems is
Gerry Gilbert

it was a 3-Vladimir reading, I mean
Calgary is bigger than Alberta I mean
Calgary is a flash in the panic I mean
you can do what you can in Calgary I mean
but in Alberta you gotta do what you got I mean
peace is bigger than war I mean
the poem is bigger than the story I mean
the drunks begging at the front door of the Glenbow Museum
  and the top floor collection of weapons
  and the art in the middle of the war
  are smaller than the...
  the...
  I mean...
the vision, the way you see, see even this I mean
Calgary makes me younger than any other city I mean
open faced I mean
Calgary has critical mass I mean
Alberta has an uncritical mask I mean
57% voted the Cons into 90% of the seats I mean
you mean a lot to me I mean
you expect poetry

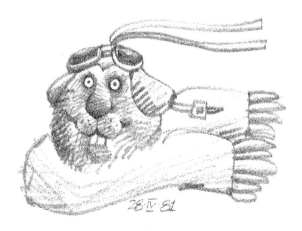

All My Nephews Have Gone to the Tar Sands
Colleen Thibaudeau

All my nephews have gone to the Tar Sands.
I find it difficult to write to them.
One slept in his truck all winter
40 below and no postal code.
One helpless watched his little farm-girl wife
Let the home-sick tears freeze into terrible silence.
One fathered what I nickname
The Tar Sands Baby. I'm wondering,
Nephews, is what I feel writing you neon letters
The same feeling maybe that my grandma had
When she would turn and look out the window,
(Staring just above the frostline & geraniums)
Her voice flat & inevitable: "They've gone to the West."
All my nephews have gone to the Tar Sands.
I find it difficult to write to them.

A Canadian Is Somebody Who
John Robert Colombo

Thinks he knows how to make love in a canoe
Bets on the Toronto Maple Leafs
Enjoys Air Canada dinners, desserts and all
Distinguishes between Wayne and Shuster
Attends the concerts of Anne Murray and Liona Boyd
Boasts Donald Sutherland was born in New Brunswick
Possesses "a sound sense of the possible"
Is sesquilingual (speaks one and a half languages)
Has become North American without becoming
Either American or Mexican
Knows what the references in this poem are all about

The Canadian Authors Meet Again

The Canadian Authors Meet
F. R. *Scott*

Expansive puppets percolate self-unction
Beneath a portrait of the Prince of Wales.
Miss Crotchet's muse has somehow failed to function,
Yet she's a poetess.   Beaming, she sails

From group to chattering group, with such a dear
Victorian saintliness, as is her fashion,
Greeting the other unknowns with a cheer —
Virgins of sixty who still write of passion.

The air is heavy with Canadian topics,
And Carman, Lampman, Roberts, Campbell, Scott,
Are measured for their faith and philanthropics,
Their zeal for God and King, their earnest thought.

The cakes are sweet, but sweeter is the feeling
That one is mixing with the *literati;*
It warms the old, and melts the most congealing.
Really, it is a most delightful party.

Shall we go round the mulberry bush, or shall
We gather at the river, or shall we
Appoint a Poet Laureate this fall,
Or shall we have another cup of tea?

O Canada, O Canada, Oh can
A day go by without new authors springing
To paint the native maple, and to plan
More ways to set the selfsame welkin ringing?

Poets & Muses
Jay Macpherson

Poets are such bad employers,
Muses ought to Organize:
Time off, sick pay, danger wages —
Come, ye wretched of the skies!

Poets, to reverse the story,
Muse-redeemed, return and live:
Solomon in all his glory
Could not pay for what you give.

Poetry for Intellectuals
Louis Dudek

If you say in a poem "grass is green,"
They all ask, "What did you mean?"

"That nature is ignorant," you reply,
"And on a deeper level — youth must die."

If you say in a poem "grass is red,"
They understand what you have said.

The Meaning of the Meaning of Poetry
Richard Sommer

I wouldn't know, being a tummy man myself

and dwelling here quietly with a girl named
Wife and a deflowered skunk called Minority
and a silver flute by the name of Tube

not to mention our tropical fish which
eat each other so fast it seems a waste
of names to call them anything at all

except stop it you

Applied Criminology
Francis Sparshott

I sit and inscribe these verses
on the back of a long proposal
to get up a master's programme
in the study of (others') crime
at the place where I make my living
I being on the committee
that decreed o sure go ahead
teach all the criminology you want
and the way I got on that committee
was being too anal-retentive
to absent myself from meetings
of things I was on already
so that all the Deans declared
here's a boy likes to go meetings
wants to be on things
so we'll put him on more things
so he can go to more meetings
so the rest of the boys can get on with their work
this is known in the teacher's trade
as a talent for administration
and gets you lots of paper
to write poems on the back of
but after all those meetings
the poems are no good

What I Shudda Said to the Lady Who Asked Me, "Shouldn't a Poet Create Beauty?"
William Bauer

Yes, Yes, Omigod, Yes!
Oh Jesus, Yes! Ogod, what else?
Rape the English dictionary from "a" to "zymurgy"
To do it if you have to,
Learn Romanian, Esperanto, Morse Code,
Blow whistles that only dogs can hear,
Lave the hands with scented soap and
Get a manicure to wigwag to the
Deaf and dumb, cock
Your ear on a lonely hillside
For a decade waiting to hear the
Music of the spheres and get it
Down in your head,
Talk back to the many-colored polished pebbles
Rolling and clicking in the streambeds
Of this lovely province,
Eavesdrop on thrashing lovers
In their heats,
Take a Famous Writer's Correspondence Course,
Blow all the little gleaming golden trumpets
There are in your soul and write down
Only the sweetest sweetest music
Of it and let the rest go by.

O lady, O beautiful lady,
Asking such a beautiful question
In this little room in a big building
Whirling along
And returning here every twenty-four hours
While I fill my lungs with tobacco smoke,
And the filaments in the electric lights
Over us crickle their way surely to darkness —
The fact of the matter is
I can't
There must be some terrible poison
In my system and I
Can't.

At Even
Wilfred Campbell

I sit me moanless in the sombre fields,
The cows come with large udders down the dusk,
One cudless, the other chewing of a husk,
Her eye askance, for that athwart her heels,
Flea-haunted and rib-cavernous, there steals
The yelping farmer-dog. An old hen sits
And blinks her eyes. (Now I must rack my wits
To find a rhyme, while all this landscape reels.)

Yes! I forgot the sky. The stars are out,
There being no clouds; and then the pensive maid!
Of course she comes with tin-pail up the lane.
Mosquitoes hum and June bugs are about.
(That line hath "quality" of loftiest grade.)
And I have eased my soul of its sweet pain.

Wasp Winter
(homage to Wilfred Campbell)
Francis Sparshott

Along the line of smoggy streets
    The crimson neon glows,
And all day long the DJ bleats
    From teenage radios.

With Nixon's news the papers groan
    Through all their dreary spread,
And all the stoplights in the town
    Have turned their green to red.

Now each with wrinkled chalky cheeks
    And vicious withered mouth
Throughout the long, cold winter weeks
    Rich birds are flying south.

A Poem for High School Anthologies

George Bowering

This will be serious, literature,
& Canadian, you'll have to look out for
the author's intentions, & also
his tricks, his puns, his jokes, the things
he is doing to make it
difficult
& hence worthwhile. Right?

Pay attention. You might be askt:
what is the most vivid figure of speech
in this selection? Just remember this:

The ivory wings of the white bird
fell off & woke the sleeping maiden
who gently lifted her feet
from the oven, piping hot!

Now you may ask yourself, what
does that symbolize, & as a matter of fact
why does the author say what
at the end of the line?

Oh, I forgot.
George Bowering was born in
Princeton, British Columbia,
December 1st, 1939, the son of
a high school Latin teacher.

There are various references to the student in this poem.
Why do you think the author keeps coming back
to that subject?

What do you think his attitude to the student is?
Pick out key words & phrases that
drive his point home.

Slave.
Lazy.
Longing for a cool mountainside & a filtertip smoke.
Forced to read a difficult poem.

She said I love you more than Mike Hunt.
Even more than reading a poem by a Canadian poet.
Does this poet know what he's doing?

How appropriate is the title?

Pullman Porter
Robert Service

The porter in the Pullman car
Was charming, as they sometimes are.
He scanned my baggage tags: "Are you
The man who wrote of Lady Lou?"
When I said "yes" he made a fuss —
Oh, he was most assiduous;
And I was pleased to think that he
Enjoyed my brand of poetry.

He was forever at my call,
So when we got to Montreal
And he had brushed me off, I said:
"I'm glad my poems you have read,
I feel quite flattered, I confess,
And if you give me your address
I'll send you (autographed, of course)
One of my little books of verse."

He smiled — his teeth were white as milk;
He spoke — his voice was soft as silk.
I recognized, despite his skin,
The perfect gentleman within.
Then courteously he made reply:
"I thank you kindly, Sir, but I
With many other cherished tome
Have all your books of verse at home.

"When I was quite a little boy
I used to savour them with joy;

And now my daughter, aged three,
Can tell the tale of Sam McGee;
While Tom, my son, that's only two,
Has heard the yarn of Dan McGrew....
Don't think your stuff I'm not applaudin' —
My taste is Eliot and Auden."

So as we gravely bade adieu
I felt quite snubbed — and so would you.
And yet I shook him by the hand,
Impressed that he could understand
The works of those two tops I mention,
So far beyond *my* comprehension —
A humble bard of boys and barmen,
Disdained, alas! by Pullman carmen.

Thoughts on Calling My Next Book "Bravo, Layton"
Irving Layton

Now my worst enemies
and the proudest men on earth
senators kings presidents MP's
as well as famous athletes and cosmonauts
will have to fall into line
with everybody else on this planet
and shout "Bravo, Layton"
when they ask for my book

Librarians book collectors and book salesmen
from Toronto all the way to Peking
will acclaim me fervently
without giving the matter a second thought
as if the huzzas were the most expected
most ordinary thing in the world

And those who hate my guts
and anyone I owe money to or a favour
all my ex-mistresses and ex-friends
                                    in fact
anyone who would like to maim or murder me
because I am famous rich sexy
generous compassionate life-loving

adored by women and children
and irrepressibly creative
will be startled out of their minds
when they're standing in a bookstore
or close to a kiosk
to hear a complete stranger
suddenly cry out, "Bravo, Layton"

Even the primmest Canucky shmuck
without reading a single line
now must begin his hostile review
by paying me homage: "Bravo, Layton"…
and though I'm too stupendously great
to have any
                    rival poets
and hordes of Canada Council poetasters
lifted from obscurity and on their way
to oblivion
will have to exclaim with everyone else
in this country, "Bravo, Layton"

Finally the terrestrial paeans
reaching him, Saint Pinchas himself
will open the pearl-studded gates
and his "Bravo, Layton"
followed by a clamorous roar of trumpets
will rebound from heaven to heaven
till the ascendant echoes
fall on the most exalted floor of all
where snoring on his onyx throne,
his sprawled-out legs glistening with constellations,
the King of Kings is roused from a post-prandial nap
that has lasted trillions and trillions
and trillions of light-years
to mumble softly into his golden beard
"Bravo, Layton…Bravo, Layton…Bravo, Layton"

Irving Layton
Ralph Gustafson

Oiving's
unnoiving.

The Terrible Word
William Bauer

The most terrible word I know
I could not bring myself to say
Or write it here on the page

It would leap to your attention
Like a turd on a white linen tablecloth

Roll around and shout at you
Until you forgot everything else
About me and my poem that is decent

For my pains
I would be forever known
As the man who put it into print
Besides I have no ambition to be called
An enemy of mankind
Or to achieve permanent notoriety at such a cost

Don't ask me what it is
I would not even whisper it
In anybody's ear much less in yours

No it is not to be found in the Bible
And it refers to no bodily function
Wholesome or perverse

It is immeasurably more bad
Than either of those things

Even in these enlightened times
I could possibly be sent to the
Electric chair for saying it

Because no one has ever been caught at it up to now
And there is no precedent yet in law
For committing such an offense

So far as I know it has only been used once
In the history of the world

In the summer of 1956
When a wholesale grocer somewhere in New Brunswick
Or maybe it was Maine
Barked his shins on the corner of
A frozen food locker

It is a God damned wonderful word

I will not tell what it is

I am saving this word

At the Quinte Hotel
Al Purdy

I am drinking
I am drinking beer with yellow flowers
in underground sunlight
and you can see that I am a sensitive man
And I notice that the bartender is a sensitive man too
so I tell him about his beer
I tell him the beer he draws
is half fart and half horse piss
and all wonderful yellow flowers
But the bartender is not quite
so sensitive as I supposed he was
the way he looks at me now
and does not appreciate my exquisite analogy
Over in one corner two guys
are quietly making love
in the brief prelude to infinity
Opposite them a peculiar fight
enables the drinkers to lay aside
their comic books and watch with interest
as I watch with interest
A wiry little man slugs another guy
then tracks him bleeding into the toilet
and slugs him to the floor again
with ugly red flowers on the tile
three minutes later he roosters over
to the table where his drunk friend sits
with another friend and slugs both
of em ass-over-electric-kettle
so I have to walk around
on my way for a piss
Now I am a sensitive man
so I say to him mildly as hell
"You shouldn'ta knocked over that good beer
with them beautiful flowers in it"
So he says to me "Come on"
so I Come On

like a rabbit with weak kidneys I guess
like a yellow streak charging
on flower power I suppose
& knock the shit outa him & sit on him
(he is just a little guy)
and say reprovingly
"Violence will get you nowhere this time chum
Now you take me
I am a sensitive man
and would you believe I write poems?"
But I could see the doubt in his upside down face
in fact in all the faces
"What kinda poems?"
"Flower poems"
"So tell us a poem"
I got off the little guy but reluctantly
for he was comfortable
and told them this poem
They crowded around me with tears
in their eyes and wrung my hands feelingly
for my pockets for
it was a heart-warming moment for Literature
and moved by the demonstrable effect
of great Art and the brotherhood of people I remarked
"— the poem oughta be worth some beer"
It was a mistake of terminology
for silence came
and it was brought home to me in the tavern
that poems will not really buy beer or flowers
or a goddam thing
and I was sad
for I am a sensitive man

Strine Authors Meet
Earle Birney

No tram   taxi dumps me on wrong side of the unknown
I climb through a maze of academic alleys   5 minutes late
blunder into a middleclass quagmire lapping up sherry

A female macaw beckons me   the local Edith Sitwell?
   Yew the kin eyejin gander gisses a lecher?
   Jus gonna read pomes
Her bill falls with alarm
   Yer nat gander read peartree? Ow long yer gan an fer?
   I allus go on till the chairman stawps me.
   Aow   (she takes my arm firmly)   yid better talk to im

We walk to the table head past place cards for 60   Cripes!
   Ow yea-yes Misser Binney   ow surrey   Misser Benny
   We been waytin fer yew
I can see the sherry's gone
An ancient fat man he sighs   but affably i think
   Rid semmena yers once about a kin eyejin fren jew add
   was killed at Deeper summers
Before I can figure that out & say thanks he's warning me
   this the Fickle Tree Club   we got to be houtbee tin
   and pipple still kemmenin   wont get stetted til Apis hate
   and henyule meeting kems festive curse
   be lucky tev affenahr fer wotayver yew intindin tew dew

We sit   The muscular arms of the lady on my right
have found a worthy opponent in the chicken
I interrupt her battle to express genuine pleasure
to see so many of the city's authors here tonight
But this one's a realist   modest too   between bites
   Affefems jis spouses   uzbints   woives   or frinze
   loike me   oim only the voice prisidents woif
I ask about the macaw down the table
   ow *err* she roits fiction   nuvvles   foive so far
She told me their names & the macaw's   nothing rang a bell

I'd slipped on my homework   Who was her publisher?
   Ow aint nennem peblished   but she's read em all to us

Nine already & still eating   Not being warned
my show was private i'd asked my young friend M
for the reading   By now he must be wandering the campus too
I told the chairman   who hadnt heard of M or of his book
(last year's winner of the national first-novel prize)
     Allem seats is pied in idvence   an allem sowld
     (He smiled) Sivn dollars a plight   Yer ena trek shun
The buggers i thought   they got me free   not even tramfare
and begrudge a chickenbone for penniless M
I tell the chairman i'm leaving to find M   He shrugs
     Iffey dan moind settin anna floor
I tell him M can have my place   I'll read standing
but just then M comes in deadpan with two young poets
They squat in the darkest back corner

The business drones on to 9.30   when the chairman introduces
a gentleman with a white goatee & stammer   who introduces
Mr. Buh-Beaney   & sits down at 9.45
The chairman huskily reminds me i've only 15 minutes
I decide to dedicate them entirely to the far corner

First a hands-across-the-commonwealth   let's make it
Frank Scott's *The Canadian Authors Meet:* "Expansive puppets..."
& now a glimpse of Canada's romantic north: Purdy's piece
about the dangers of shitting among huskies   followed by
a small statement of my own poetics: "how fucking awful
it is to be a poet" & finally a Bill Bissett "hare krishna"
chanted   walking out with the only three writers in the room

Sydney, 1968

Life on the Land Grant Review
Tom Wayman

Mad gnome of an assistant editor
Wayman gloats in Colorado
before the mass of manuscripts now his,
his to edit.

Wayman remembers the mounds of his own mail back
marked: "Are you kidding?"
"What is this grunt?" and
"Do us a favor and stick this up your ass?"

Now the tide is turned: all literary America
lies at Wayman's feet; America, with a poet
under every rock. Revenge, revenge,
the very word is like a Bedlam gong
to ring him deeper into rage...
"And that's a literary reference,"
Wayman shrieks, slashing someone's poem to
shreddies as he writes rejections
— the same for all: Miss Elsa Eddington Brewster,
editor Riley of the *South-west Pawnee County Quarterly,*
former associates with their cringing, oily letters.
Only the editor-in-chief's friends
give him pause. Wayman weighs
the first-name-basis missives carefully.
Who is putting him on? Who really studied
under Yvor with the boss? Who knew him when?
Who now? Is everybody faking?

Feverish in the cool Colorado evening
Wayman is hammering away at rejecting
faster and faster. The earth heaves,
the business manager elopes,
the editor is arrested in Utah with the funds,
still Wayman is scribbling: "No."   "No."
Imperceptibly the word spreads outward
to those in Portland, Oregon and Portland, Maine
stuffing their packages of poems
into the 10 p.m. mailbox slots:
"Wayman," the news has it,
"Wayman's editing in Colorado.
All we can do is submit."

A Chain of Haik

Robert Zend

Japanese people
think it is quite boring to
finish their senten

I agree with them
we can guess anyway what
should come after the

We go to bed when
we are sleepy and not when
we finished what we

We die the same way
there are many unfinished
things to do when sud

Western reader, I
hope you will understand me,
and if not, you can

How to Become a Fashionable Writer
David Donnell

Change your birth certificate. Become 17.
Move to a large urban center and attend university.
Wear slightly outré clothes. Smoke Gitanes.
Read Dostoievski and make profound comments about the novel.
Ask your professors: "Is this relevant to our real experience?"
Buy most of your books at stores downtown.
Live on campus for part of first year
but get a seedy apartment for the rest of your degree.
Go out with a girl from the art college.
Do not own pets.
Complain about a lack of light at the Graduate Center.
Defend the college baseball team
by saying you think they're frustrated artists.
Tell people that your parents live somewhere interesting
like New York or San Francisco or Paris or Amsterdam.
Invent a wealthy uncle who lives in North York.
Visit him on Tuesdays when you have nothing else to do.
Avoid being seen in the college library
but stop by occasionally for conversations on the front steps.
Do not buy a car. Do not walk around with a knapsack.
Claim to be interested in the NDP but avoid going to meetings.
Patronize a good cheap restaurant at least once a month.
Refer to the Rolling Stones as the flagship of the 70's.
Be late with all your papers because you were too busy
listening to Mahler to be bothered writing the crap.
Be seen going in and out of Le Strip. Avoid being seen inside.
Buy an expensive leather shoulder bag but don't wear it.
Send poems to good magazines but not every week.
Write to people like William Burroughs.
Go to a lot of Fellini films but balance them with Altman.
Be clean-shaven so you can show up occasionally with a stubble.
Get your hair cut regularly. Wear white in the summer.
Publish your first novel before you're 21.

Hope John Cale records one of your songs. Circulate rumors
that you're becoming a Catholic because you enjoy mass.
Try not to get arrested. Get arrested for angel dust.
Write at least ten great poems.
Be non-committal with interviewers but smile at the audience.
Do not appear on a seals program. Do not eat seals.
Do not move to the country. Avoid getting drunk at parties.
Never publish a collected poems.
If hard pressed for a second novel, publish an intelligent journal.

from *Transcanadaletters*
Roy Kiyooka

Dear Susan

Mus(k) grave: Permit *the mushroom*
in me to say to the woman you are   that
your gift of the magical elixir is
is ISIS the Egyptian goddess and patron
saint of the movie house by that name
on 1st Street West between 11th and 12th
avenue in Calgary Alta I attended as
a 30s lad. Even today I can see I S I S
pronounced 'I'-siz   flashing frm
the marquee. And if for whatever reason
you dont or wont let this Egyptian
bird speak in and thru you you nonetheless
deserve Her. Dear mushroom-giver its
hightime you also took some of whatever
the Queen Charlottes (AWESOMELY) gives to
even a mushroom/ sez the rain forest
Dwarf who tends them w/ love.

        wonder how Gulliver wld have
        dealt w/ it after eating a bushel?

The Future of Poetry in Canada
Elizabeth Brewster

Some people say we live in a modern mechanized nation
where the only places that matter
are Toronto, Montreal, and maybe Vancouver;
but I myself prefer Goodridge, Alberta,
a town where electricity arrived in 1953,
the telephone in 1963.

In Goodridge, Alberta
the most important social events
have been the golden wedding anniversaries of the residents.
There have been a Garden Club, a Junior Grain Club, and
    a Credit Union,
and there have been farewell parties,
well attended in spite of the blizzards.

Weather is important in Goodridge.
People remember the time they threshed in the snow,
and the winter the temperature fell to seventy below.

They also remember the time
the teacher from White Rat School
piled eight children in his car
and drove them, as a treat,
all the way to Edmonton;
where they admired the Jubilee Auditorium
and the Parliament Buildings
and visited the CNR wash rooms
but were especially thrilled
going up and down in an elevator.

I hope at least one poet
in the next generation
comes from Goodridge, Alberta.

Getting On with It
Sharon Thesen

The word
Shakespeare
reaches upstairs from CBC
I shiver, don't feel
so good. Poetry,
4:50 PM & this
curtained light.
Shakespeare
drag yr mouldy old bones
up these stairs & tell me
what you died of,
I think
I've got it
too.

In Public Places

First Political Speech
Eli Mandel

first, in the first place, to begin with, secondly,
in the second place, lastly

again, also, in the next place, once more, moreover,
furthermore, likewise, besides, similarly, for example,
for instance, another

then, nevertheless, still, however, at the same time,
yet, in spite of that, on the other hand, on the contrary

certainly, surely, doubtless, indeed, perhaps, possibly,
probably, anyway, in all probability, in all likelihood,
at all events, in any case

therefore, consequently, accordingly, thus, as a result,
in consequence of this, as might be expected

the foregoing, the preceding, as previously mentioned

as already stated

"Transition Table"
from *Learning to Write* by Ernest
H. Winter (Second Revised Edition)
Macmillan (Toronto, 1961), p. 156.

Routines

Tom Wayman

After a while the body doesn't want to work.
When the alarm clock rings in the morning
the body refuses to get up. "You go to work if you're so keen,"
it says. "Me, I'm going back to sleep."
I have to nudge it in the ribs to get it out of bed.
If I had my way I'd just leave you here, I tell it
as it stands blinking. *But I need you to carry your end of the load.*
I take the body into the bathroom
intending to start the day as usual with a healthy dump.
But the body refuses to perform.
Come on, come on, I say between my teeth.
Produce, damn you. It's getting late.
"Listen, this is all your idea," the body says.
"If you want some turds so badly you provide 'em.
I'd just as soon be back in bed."
I give up, flush, wash, and go make breakfast.
Pretty soon I'm at work. All goes smoothly enough
until the first break. I open my lunchpail
and start to munch on some cookies and milk.
"Cut that out," the body says, burping loudly.
"It's only a couple of hours since breakfast.
And two hours from this will be lunch, and two hours after that
will be the afternoon break. I'm not a machine
you can force-feed every two hours.
And it was the same yesterday, too..."
I hurriedly stuff an apple in its mouth to shut it up.

By four o'clock the body is tired
and even more surly. It will hardly speak to me
as I drive home. I bathe it, let it lounge around.
After supper it regains some of its good spirits.
But as soon as I get ready for bed it starts to make trouble.
Look, I tell it, *I've explained this over and over.*
I know it's only ten o'clock but we have to be up in eight hours.
If you don't get enough rest, you'll be dragging around all day
tomorrow again, cranky and irritable.

"I don't care," the body says. "It's too early.
When do I get to have any fun? If you want to sleep
go right ahead. I'm going to lie here wide awake
until I feel good and ready to pass out."

It is hours before I manage to convince it to fall asleep.
And only a few hours after that the alarm clock sounds again.
"Must be for you," the body murmurs. "You answer it."
The body rolls over. Furious, and without saying a word,
I grab one of its feet and begin to yank it toward the edge of the bed.

The Halfmoon Bay Improvement Society
Florence McNeil

The Halfmoon Bay Improvement Society
meets every Thursday night
in Welcome Beach Hall
the delegates playing their starched tunes
ignore
the sounds of squirrels running
and the seagulls and pigeons who take turns
on the roof
Mrs. Pringle who substituted watering cans
for trees
and bulldozed a hill of hippies
is in the chair
the pressure of her stare freezes crows
into silence
tea is poured
the vicar's smile rises like a sea moon
while along the starry coastline rusty pipes
inch like worms into the ocean
and the pungent smell of Halfmoon Bay's
low tide
ascends to the heavens.

The Royal Visit
James Reaney

When the King and the Queen came to Stratford
Everyone felt at once
How heavy the Crown must be.
The Mayor shook hands with their Majesties
And everyone presentable was presented
And those who weren't have resented
It, and will
To their dying day.
Everyone had almost a religious experience
When the King and Queen came to visit us
(I wonder what they felt!)
And hydrants flowed water in the gutters
All day.
People put quarters on the railroad tracks
So as to get squashed by the Royal Train
And some people up the line at Shakespeare
Stayed in Shakespeare, just in case —
They did stop too,
While thousands in Stratford
Didn't even see them
Because the Engineer didn't slow down
Enough in time.
And although,
But although we didn't see them in any way
(I didn't even catch the glimpse
The teacher who was taller did
Of a gracious pink figure)
I'll remember it to my dying day.

In the Basement
Christopher Wiseman

Check the laundry room
during the day and you'll see them,
washer and dryer, standing quietly
next to each other, a matched pair
minding their own business.
At night it's different.
Under the complacent sleep
of this Calgary suburb
something strange is going on.

It's not surprising.
Think of their frustration
standing day after day
with bare white flanks touching
each throbbing with power
but programmed separately.
No wonder they go mad
when we're not there.

Exactly what they do we don't know —
genial couplings with hoses
switches and cords;
clumsy titanic orgies —
we have never disturbed them.
All we know is that in the mornings
beads of cooling moisture
stand on their gleaming sides,
the basement air is warm,
and on the floor
confused marks of castors
and a sinister trace of suds.

One night perhaps we shall creep
down and surprise them.
But now, our claim to the house less,
we go to bed earlier and earlier.

Overheard at a Taxpayers' Meeting
Francis Sparshott

Mr. Alderman it's about the old people's home there
they're getting out all the time
something will have to be done about it
it's not nice

They sneak out the back way and prowl around the grounds
and as soon as a person opens the gate
the ambulance maybe or a delivery van or the lads from the funeral home
they're off you can't stop them they're quick they're artful
that's all they have to think about getting away
they sit together in the corners and scheme
when they're supposed to be drinking their cocoa
the moment the head nurse gets a headache and goes to lie down
that's it they swarm out the windows
it's like an anthill
stepstools tables kitchenchairs benches
ropes too I wouldn't wonder
I bet they use ropes
there's no keeping them back

I was talking last night to the guard at the school crossing
he was in shock
a covey of grannies in slippers and mohair shawls
bald as the back of your hand
took over his crossing they wouldn't wait for his flag
staggering and wheezing all over the highway
traffic was backed up half way to West Hill
it's not right

It's getting so people don't know what to expect
you can't keep them out of the garden
I daren't look in the shrubbery
for fear that a drove of escaped senior citizens
will have up and died on me overnight
and who pays to clear them away just tell me that
while here we are trying to upgrade the neighbourhood
well it's disheartening

The nurses are run ragged
of course they're understaffed who isn't understaffed
if they guard one exit the old devils slip out the other
old men improperly dressed on the public streets
flashing striped cotton pyjamas at innocent kids
well maybe a jersey
you have to call the fire department and the St. Vincent de Paul
to get some clothes on them
it isn't a thing respectable people want to see
a lot of old people like that
it's not decent

I came home lateish the other evening
humming the goodbye theme from Wayne and Shuster
it had been a long day I was looking forward to that martini
there was an old person in the kitchen
munching at the fridge
chicken or brisket or ken-l-ration
it's all one to them with their energetic old gums
what they can't chew they mumble
well I had to send for the cops I mean to say
took them an hour to get here
and there was I with an old person in the house
it's not what we have a right to expect
why do we pay taxes

If you leave a downstairs window open only a bare crack
they're in like a shot
dragging their old soft bones in over the sill
trailing canes and crutches
we find them clustered squatting around the TV
watching reruns of Queen for a Day and This Is Your Life
muttering incomprehensible curses

We tell the kids not to go near the place
to tell the truth we don't like it either
feeling those gummy eyes on your back
a gate creaks behind you
and you hear a grunting and a tapping of sticks
why can't they build a big wall with spikes
they could bar the windows
it wasn't to have them scattering all over Metro
their families paid good money to have them put away
in Sunset Acres.

In the Supermarket
Ken Norris

I am in the supermarket
                surveying
The prospects of the dairy section
When a female hand
                  darts out
Of nowhere
And quickly plucks
         a huge round of gouda cheese
From the shelf.
I am astounded —
        the cheese is above my means.
I turn to observe
        the face of the fortunate lady
Who can afford such extravagance.
She is a pigtailed beauty
Wrapped in a leather coat.
My emotions rise:
I love her and her cheese.

Quickly she is off, pushing
Her cart before I can say a word.
So I go on shopping.
I cool my passion by perusing
A section of frozen foods.
But later, over turnips, we meet again.
My love grows
Among the fruits and vegetables.
I decide to hold an asparagus
        between my teeth
And dance with the flash of a flamenco;
But she disappears again
After taking advice from a counterman
About raisins.

I go back to my purchasing.
I squeeze a tomato, caress an eggplant,
Get excited about the price of lettuce.

In the bread section I decide
That if we ever meet again
           I will give her a potato
To show my affection.
If she accepts it
           we will stroll through the store,
Our purchases in one mutual cart,
           and sing praises
To the A & P,
           our divine matchmaker.
We will be like apple pie and ice cream,
           pork and beans,
Baked potato and sour cream.
And I came here looking for food!
Bah, mere sustenance!
In this atmosphere of plenty
I have found love!

I remember that she has vanished among the aisles.
I look for her in soups, cereals, salad dressings;
She is not there.
On to meats, cookies, spices;
                         Alas!
In despair
           I decide to check out;
She stands before me,
Emptying her cart out onto the conveyor.
She moves with such grace.
I observe the bounty of her cart.
She has cans of cat food,
A sure sign of loneliness.
Besides the cheese
           which brought her
Into my blood
She has minor items.
She has an eggplant wrapped in cellophane.
My cart contains one too:
A common affinity.
A jar of meat sauce, stewed tomatoes.
She plays with a pigtail as she waits.
The check-out girl is slow.

My love speaks to the girl in the language of the land;
Perhaps they briefly discuss Quebec appetites.
I cannot tell; I am not a delicate crepe
Nor a stocky bouillabaise; I'm an English stew,
Worse than that, American,
A hamburger with french fries and a coke.

My heart sinks.
Her total is soon added,
The items placed in bags.
She pays and turns to leave.
I want to call out to her a recipe,
A helpful hint about spaghetti, anything.

Too late, too late.
All the way home
I long for her company at dinner.

In Addition
Milton Acorn

In addition to the fact I lost my job for a nosebleed

In addition to the fact my unemployment insurance stamps were just
    one week short

In addition to the fact I'm standing in line at the Sally Ann for a
    breakfast of one thin baloney sandwich and coffee

In addition to all that it's lousy coffee.

Edmonton Centre, Sept. 23/80
Phyllis Webb

It was just there. It? They? Music
suddenly I come upon the
                                    key cutting shop
and "Wool" and a young bassist — bronzed hair long
beyond her waist
                        Music
in the courtyard of the Centre. One can smoke
and listen to Music with little kids
lying on stomachs
                        escalator climbing with surprised
mid-day Edmontonians playing it cool
              who look askance
                            or turn around as the
Music mounts with them into leafy levels
of Marks and Spencers
                        staring —
The Edmonton Symphony in plain clothes fiddling
the bad vibes of Eatons and Woodwards, key shop
grinding out keys.
                  Keys!
And after the final number I'm sure I see
Maureen Forrester licking a vanilla ice-cream cone
— she waves her musical hand to a friend in the winds.
Man in cowboy hat wanders off. Chinese gentleman
moves urgently towards "Exit." Maureen takes
the escalator, strolls into Mappins.

Touchstone. She is touchstone. Remember Maureen
the Trout Quintet that summer of '51 in Montreal?

But maybe it isn't Forrester, after all. Thirty
years later, almost, I am here
carrying nonbiodegradable plastic shopping bags
back
           to the scarey carpark
                        jangling my keys

The Opener
Raymond Souster

From where I was sitting
it looked like an easy double-play.

But at that precise moment
a sloppy looking freighter
slipped into the Western Gap
with a clothesline of washing
half the length of her deck,

and the runner going into second
took one look at that ship
and yelled: "Hey, look, they got
my old lady's black pants
flying at the masthead."

And when all the infield
turned around to get a gape,
he made second, stole third,
and scored standing up
the winning run in what otherwise
was one of the cleanest-played openers
in a Toronto ball-park.

The Football Match
Anonymous

I

O wild kaleidoscopic panorama of jaculatory arms and legs.
The twisting, twining, turning, tussling, throwing, thrusting,
    throttling, tugging, thumping, the tightening thews.
The tearing of tangled trousers, the jut of giant calves protuberant.
The wriggleness, the wormlike, snaky movement and life of it;
The insertion of strong men in the mud, the wallowing, the stamping with
    thick shoes;
The rowdyism, and *élan*, the slugging and scraping, the cowboy Homeric
    ferocity.
(Ah, well kicked, red legs! Hit her up, you muddy little hero, you!)
The bleeding noses, the shins, the knuckles abraded:
That's the way to make men! Go it, you border ruffians, I like ye.

II

Only two sorts of men are any good, I wouldn't give a cotton hat for no
        other —
The Poet and the Plug Ugly. They are picturesque. Oh, but ain't they?
These college chaps, these bouncing fighters from M'Gill and Toronto,
Are all right. I must have a fighter, a bully, somewhat of a desperado;
Of course, I prefer them raw, uneducated, unspoiled by book rot;
I reckon these young fellows, these howling Kickapoos of the puddle, these
        boys,
Have been uneducated to an undemocratic and feudal-aristocratic extent;
Lord! how they can kick, though! Another man slugged there!

III

Unnumbered festoons of pretty Canadian girls, I salute you;
Howl away, you non-playing encouragers of the kickers!
Rah, Rah, Rah, Rah, Rah, Rah, M'Gill!
Rah, Rah, Rah, Sis, Boom, Toronto! Lusty-throated give it!
Oh, wild, tumultuous, multitudinous shindy. Well, this is the boss;
This is worth coming twenty miles to see. Personally, I haven't had so much
        fun since I was vaccinated.
I wonder if the Doctor spectates it. Here is something beyond his plesiosauri.
Purely physical glow and exultation this of abundantest muscle:
I wish John Sullivan were here.

IV

Oh, the kicking, stamping, punching, the gore and the glory of battle!
Kick, kick, kick, kick, kick, kick. *Will* you kick!
You kickers, scoop up the mud, steam plough the field,
Fall all over yourselves, squirm out! Look at that pile-driver of a full-back there!
Run, leg it, hang on to the ball; say, you big chump, don't you kill that little
        chap
When you are about it.
Well, I'd like to know what a touchdown is, then? Draw?
Where's your draw?
Yer lie!

Once Is Once Too Many
Stephen Scriver

I only forgot to wear my can
once   that was enough

it was one time over in Glenavon
I went out for my first shift
and you know how when you're waiting
for the drop of the puck
you lean over and rest
your stick across your can
well, this time all I can feel
is wide-open spaces and the family jewels

but I'm not gonna skate
back to the bench
so I figger I'll get
by for this shift anyways

well, I'm all over the ice
like a mad man's shit and
I chase the puck into their corner
pass it back to Brian on defence
then head for the net to screen the goalie

when I look back to the point
sure as God's got sandals
Brian's just blasted one crotch-high

not to worry I figger
I'll just jump and let it cruise
between my legs

well, I couldn'ta timed'er
more perfect   it was just
like a three-ball combination

cept that two of them were damn
near in my throat
while the puck caroms into the net
like snot off a door knob

was I pleased?
is the Pope married?

The Hustlers
Glen Sorestad

Forrie and I have held the pool table
at the Jan Lake bar for too long now
it's plain to see
There are mutters, hard glances
begrudged dollar bills
stacked on our table, an untidy pile
while we reel in our fortune
like sailors on shore leave

But Ernie has already lost twice to us
and now prompted by two whites
slams the cue ball into a pocket
(a move that is far from friendly)
knowing that his opponent must hit
the black ball shooting up and down
using one of the sloppy cushions
or lose the game

I must face this ploy
and I know it's no joke
not just a shot to leave me tough
It's a warning to Forrie and me
that we've been here long enough
and we'd be wise to pack it in

Every eye in the place is on me
to see how well we've paid attention
and the sudden silence is deafening
as I step to the table to shoot

So I listen carefully — and miss the shot

There's a happy explosion of table-talk
We pay off Ernie and his partner
and Ernie averts our eyes:
he's had more satisfying victories

but we've listened so well
(and like the sight of our own blood so little)
that we take our stack of ones and buy beer
send it around to the tables of losers
and a much more healthy hum
fills the smoky air when we sit down
and we know we won't have to listen
for footsteps behind us when we leave

The Poet Is Bidden to Manhattan Island
Sir Charles G. D. Roberts

Dear Poet, quit your shady lanes
    And come where more than lanes are shady.
Leave Phyllis to the rustic swains
    And sing some Knickerbocker lady.
O hither haste, and here devise
    Divine *ballades* before unuttered.
Your poet's eyes *must* recognize
    The side on which your bread is buttered!

Dream not I tempt you to forswear
    One pastoral joy, or rural frolic.
I call you to a city where
    The most urbane are most bucolic.
'Twill charm your poet's eyes to find
    Good husbandmen in brokers burly; —
Their stock is ever on their mind;
    To water it they rise up early.

Things you have sung, but ah, not seen —
    Things proper to the age of Saturn —
Shall greet you here; for we have been
    Wrought quaintly, on the Arcadian pattern.
Your poet's lips will break in song
    For joy, to see at last appearing
The bulls and bears, a peaceful throng,
    While a lamb leads them — to the shearing!

And metamorphoses, of course,
  You'll mark in plenty, *à la* Proteus:
A bear become a little horse —
  Presumably from too much throat-use!
A thousandfold must go untold;
  But, should you miss your farm-yard sunny,
And miss your ducks and drakes, behold
  We'll make you ducks and drakes — of money!

Greengrocers here are fairly read.
  And should you set your heart upon them,
We lack not beets — but some are dead,
  While others have policemen on them.
And be the dewfall dear to you,
  Possess your poet's soul in patience!
Your *notes* shall soon be falling dew, —
  Most mystical of transformations!

Your heart, dear Poet, surely yields;
  And soon you'll leave your uplands flowery,
Forsaking fresh and bowery fields,
  For 'pastures new' — upon the Bowery!
You've piped at home, where none could pay,
  Till now, I trust, your wits are riper.
Make no delay, but come this way,
  And pipe for them that pay the piper!

The Throwback Voice

R. G. *Everson*

Although my voice has lived in Canada since 1792
when my grandmother (some removes) walked with her
    children
from northern Vermont to Niagara-on-the-Lake,
my flat voice fits only in northern Vermont.

When I first visited that state I had no expectation
of finding a home for my voice. I clambered around
the north side of Smugglers' Notch in a spring morning,
but found the pass still plugged with snow.

In the valley the Lamoille River was in spate.
I walked down and sat resting on a log.
An old man came along. I said, "Quite a flood."
"Taint a patch to '27," he replied. And I remembered
    reading
of the big flood, 1927. He said, "You mind
how it took out the grist mill and them three houses.
Nobody got hurted. The Power Company had to pay."

Later, to get some cheese and wintered apples for my lunch,
I climbed to a general store. As he passed me the change
and the food, the storekeeper said, "Quite a flood."
"Taint a patch to '27," I replied.
My voice brought the storekeeper around
his counter. And three other men appeared
from behind some packing crates. The one with the straw
dangling from his mouth, invited me, "Tell us more,
old timer." I had little script remaining
and I feared to add anything lest I lose
whatever peculiar quality my voice might have.

So I said, "You mind how it took out the grist mill.
And them three houses. Nobody got hurted.
The Power Company had to pay."

I bowed to my admiring audience, as the storekeeper
opened the door for me and I went with my cheese
and wintered apples into the hills nearby
where they probably think I have lived forever.

On Meeting the Clergy
of the Holy Catholic Church in Osaka
Joy Kogawa

Heralded into a belly swelling bladder bloating banquet
Where the excessive propriety is hard on the digestion
Elegant ladies in kimonos and holy men with holier manners
Bow and re-bow in strict pecking order
Munch the meal and mouth polite belching and
Rush at flood tide to the integrated toilet
Where men still proper and black suited in a row
Stand toes out and eyes down in syncopated gush
While ladies in kimonos mince by without blush or bellow
And I follow snuffling to hide a guffaw though
Why I should laugh — which reminds me
At the Osaka zoo my friend kept pointing out
The peeing fox and the baboon's purple bum and such
Asking how to say these things in English
And I tried to explain about the odd Canadians
Who have no bread and butter words
To describe these ordinary things.

Greeks Had Nothing Else to Do
R. G. Everson

An ancient Greek awoke at dawn
shook loose his blanket which he then put on
draping it elegantly around him for a cloak
Unhindered by TV radio books newspaper
or breakfast, which he did not have, he went out

against no traffic. Little wonder
an Athenian soon got to work. It was right there,
near home. When he returned at night
the classic soil, stripped bare, classic light,
did not impose on him lawn-mowing
Also, Greeks didn't go in for women-wooing

With nothing else to do, even I might romp,
inventing choral odes, all literature
and thought, or run a footrace or a war
against my city's state of Persian pomp

Rutabagas
David Donnell

The first step to be taken on the rutabaga market is simple.
Buy up all the cheap rutabaga producers and sit on them.
Then introduce rutabagas to the Toronto market at $2.00 a pound.
Run some large magazine spreads on rutabagas. Talk about their history.
Gradually drop the price to about $1.50 a pound.
"Rutabagas become popular." Begin to market them seriously.
Run spreads on prestigious people who like to eat rutabagas.
Actors will probably want their rutabagas chopped up with soy.
Vegetarians will want their rutabagas boiled with spinach.
Rutabaga pie may become very popular. Rutabaga and steak.
This is the way to make people happy. This is the way to make money.
Soon almost everyone will take rutabagas for granted. Wonderful.
Now raise the price of rutabagas very slowly to about $3.00 a pound.
Amazing. Two years ago they'd never heard of rutabagas.
Now they're in love with this unusual vegetable and can't live without it.
Great.
Who knows what rutabagas are? They want them.
Maybe a new rutabaga can be introduced. A lighter rutabaga.
A more chemically attuned rutabaga for approximately $3.45 a pound.
Great. And everyone is happy and goes to the market.
I am some distance away in all of this. Removed.
I sit in my office and read the newspapers. I smoke cigars.
When rutabagas go to $3.75 a pound I cannot contain myself.
I throw my newspapers in the garbage and make love to my secretary
over the desk with the day's correspondence falling all over the floor.
I am a success. I am the rutabaga king of North America.
I am so excited I can hardly do up my pants.
A pale frightened man with a cigar and a back problem.
I go down in the elevator glowing with pride.
Rutabagas. I can't stand them. They taste like musty turnips.
The very thought of them makes me sick to my stomach.
I barf in an ashcan and go home and listen to Berg
and write a poem about the formal structure of trees.

The Silent Poet at Intermission
Robert Kroetsch

but   who are all these strangers, I ask
and   I mean it, heading for the bar
but   trust my luck, Earache the Red, a drink in either
        hand, announces, Madame Sosostris has a bad cold this
        evening, we laugh
and   I say, that's pharoah enough
but   nobody gets it, I buy my own
and   Earache, the crowd gathering, art should instruct,
        he tells us, glancing at his reflection
but   not by painting the rainbow black, we laugh
and   I have a pot myself, Labatt's did that much for me
but   she who loves gold loves elsewhere
and   follows the path prophesying no end, it's hardly hard
        to guess; uppie uppie, she says in the morning, the
        medium well done
but   he hands her a glass, she looks; here's mud in your
        eye
and   even The Virgin Queen, she wasn't Shakespeare either
But   I did scorn them all, she wrote
and   with good cause: a leman is a lemon, ha; well, let the
        heads fall
but   music, he says, is the mothering lode; he waves his
        arms; he is composing a series of dichotomies for
        violin
and   fiddle, the chiseling clod
but   he spills his drink
and   I wipe my shoe on my cuff; I hear the weasel that sniffs
        the hen, the blood-loud blood in the gutter, the wise
        man strangling on his own; sorry, mum
but   he discovers, just then, the split of mind
and   body; putting Descartes before the hearse, we laugh
but   just as I raise the dagger the buzzer sounds, I am
        left with the thought in my hand
and   he takes her elbow in his palm; the new, he tells us,
        straight to our backs, must learn to be old, to learn
        to be new; we scratch ourselves
but   follow, as we lead, to the first usher
and   I leave for home, bumping knees with a dozen strangers
but   never go

Harry, 1967
John Newlove

Old Harry just sits on the porch all day staring at himself and not seeing a damn thing.

Or to tell the truth he doesn't even sit on the porch. His house hasn't got a porch.

Or to tell the truth Harry hasn't got a house.

Harry lives in a ten-dollar-a-week light-housekeeping room and thinks of himself sitting on the porch of a house he never had.

Harry has become very familiar with oatmeal and macaroni in his old age. He is thirty-six, born in 1931.

Born after the First World War, born after the twenties, born just in time to barely remember a small portion of the Depression, born too young to fight in the Second World War, to remember details really well.

Harry is five foot seven and a half, Harry weighs one hundred and thirty pounds, Harry has dandruff, Harry has bad teeth and no prospect of ever getting them fixed, Harry wears glasses, Harry quit school at sixteen before he finished Grade Nine to get in on the big money.

Harry looks like he's had TB all his life but Harry hasn't, Harry has nothing and looks like getting less.

But Harry sits on that porch all day feeling the sunlight almost and not seeing a damn thing. It's been a lousy life and it's only just half over.

Harry is thirty-six and he doesn't even dream about women anymore. Harry knows he'll never touch a woman again.

So what's the use of thinking about it.

But Harry used to see things.

Harry went to Ethiopia and was a general in a revolution.

And he killed the emperor with his own hand.

And his gallant tribesmen swept down upon the lines of khaki machine-gunmen and sabred every one of them.

Harry was nicked by a fragment of shell that left an inch-long cut like one a knife would make on his forearm.

And Harry had no expression on his face when he removed the cigarette from his mouth and used its burning tip to cauterize the wound while fat newspapermen gasped in admiration as the faint smell of toasted flesh reached them.

And the movie cameras whirred.

And Harry waved his sword and ordered his cavalry to charge and all around the world movie audiences watching the Movietone News gasped as Harry slaughtered the old Emperor himself and his admiring tribesmen crowned Harry king and Harry. . . .

Harry always thought the word was calvary not cavalry, legacy of a short time at Sunday School in the damp cloakroom of a prairie United Church.

That was a long time ago to Harry and he has a long time to go.

And Harry doesn't see anymore.

He doesn't know that it's useless to see things that can never happen, he doesn't know that for him dreaming is just a lie now, that seeing things is no good for him, too late: that isn't why Harry doesn't see.

Harry just can't anymore, that's all.

Today I am thirty-nine
Douglas Lochhead

Today I am thirty-nine
so what, who cares,
what else is new?

Spring rides on a robin,
I saw him in the loose earth
where the houses were torn down,
now a thawed worm fills
his throat, but look away,
the ear hears the round first notes
forgetting the worm.

To draw lessons, after all this past
these thirty-nine, these steps,
a race, a crawl, intrigue,
beginning as is customary
with birth, a dirty city day like this
in Guelph where they still make pickles
and at the College, horse-doctors.

No lessons, the raw raw youth
playing hockey with horseballs
on the road in Ottawa,
McGill and the thawing rest...
O where O where
and now my daughters new
from their beds surround me
and outsing the robin's
Happy Birthday to you.

This past I take, tomorrow
sits on another fence,
today I am thirty-nine
and I think I will go to Eatons
and even Simpsons to celebrate
with my credit cards.

Destiny
Leonard Cohen

I want your warm body to disappear
politely and leave me alone in the bath
because I want to consider my destiny.
Destiny! why do you find me in this bathtub,
idle, alone, unwashed, without even
the intention of washing except at the last moment?
Why don't you find me at the top of a telephone pole,
repairing the lines from city to city?
Why don't you find me riding a horse through Cuba,
a giant of a man with a red machete?
Why don't you find me explaining machines
to underprivileged pupils, negroid Spaniards,
happy it is not a course in creative writing?
Come back here, little warm body,
it's time for another day.
Destiny has fled and I settle for you
who found me staring at you in a store
one afternoon four years ago
and slept with me every night since.
How do you find my sailor eyes after all this time?
Am I what you expected?
Are we together too much?
Did Destiny shy at the double Turkish towel,
our knowledge of each other's skin,
our love which is a proverb on the block,
our agreement that in matters spiritual
I should be the Man of Destiny
and you should be the Woman of the House?

Out of the Mouths...

Stefan
P. K. Page

Stefan
aged eleven
looked at the baby and said
When he thinks it must be pure thought
because he hasn't any words yet
and we
proud parents
admiring friends
who had looked at the baby

looked at the baby again

A True Poem
David McFadden

Seeing, hearing & smelling said six-year-old Alison
when asked what she liked best about life,
making the Philosophers look kind of silly.

Alex
Phyllis Webb

at five o'clock today Alex four years old said

I will draw a picture of you!

at first he gave me no ears and I said

you should give me ears

I would like big ears one on each side

and he added them and three buttons down the front

now I'll make your skirt wide he said and he did

and he put pins in all up and down my ribs and I waited

and he said now I'll put a knife in you

it was in my side and I said does it hurt

and No! he said and we laughed and he said

now I'll put a fire on you and he put male

fire on me in the right place then scribbled me

all into flames shouting FIRE FIRE FIRE

FIRE FIRE FIRE and I said

shall we call the fire engines and he said Yes!

this is where they are and the ladders are bending

and we made siren noises as he drew the engines on

over the page then he said the Hose! and he put

the fire out and that's better I said

and he rolled over laughing like crazy

because it was all on paper

1949
Craig Powell

When I was eight years
old I showed my bum
to Melody Forsyte   giggling in
a backyard shed   in the
musky scrub of vacant
allotments   by pools
in fern gullies where we dipped
our jars for tadpoles too   I
bared my shy
and wicked bum to Melody
Forsyte   who showed me
hers
              when I was
eight   in my grandmother's
fig trees we dangled like
flying foxes   her lewd little
knees were scabbed and scraped
with soil   and my eyes
hop-scotched from her knees
to her panties   all
childhood a twinkling
of bums   in branches the stars
swam into   but she never revealed
that dark sweet cleft
of her groin   and I
hid in my thighs one
furtive   drooping
bruisable Narcissus flower

In a puzzled land   in the Frog
Prince dream after World War II
I was eight years old   I yielded
respect to my parents   my
heart for the Lord Jesus Christ but
my bum to Melody Forsyte

Capitalism
Leona Gom

The first four years
I rode horseback to school,
        most of the other kids
        coming in by then
        some other way,
        in something motorized
        but less reliable.

So there I was
with the only horse at school,
and it had started to become that time
when horses were a novelty
to my tractor-jaded generation,
and I soon realized
I had a good thing here.

At recess I set up my business:
        a penny a pat
        a nickel a ride
        a dime for the whole noon hour.
There were mishaps, of course,
but generally minor,
        resulting mostly from the horse
        thinking it was home time
        and heading eagerly off,
but this seemed only to add
to the thrill.

Business was good,
and word got around.
Eventually it reached my parents,
and I was ordered to stop,
which even then seemed contrary
to the free-enterprise ethic
I was learning elsewhere, everywhere.
But I was hardly in position
to oppose this government intervention,
so I closed my barn doors,
burned the books,
and that was that.

I confess
to a certain nostalgia
for that early entrepreneur,
having never since
been so successfully self-employed.

Grade Five Geography Lesson
Barry Stevens

Children never get to the point,
They surround it.
The importance of the point
Is the landscape of it.
You begin by discussing
"The Rainfall of Vancouver Island"
And somebody has an uncle who lives there.
And there is an uncle in Alberta
Who has a zillion cows,
Some chickens and a horse
(We get to feed the chickens
And ride the horse),
Which brings us to an uncle
In Saskatchewan, who has a house where
Deer pass the kitchen window
Every morning (He takes us out
And shows us where they go).
If there were no uncles on Vancouver Island
It would never rain there.

The Long Summer Afternoon
William Bauer

"Let's open a lemonade stand," cried Jane
"Let's not," said Dick
"I know," cried Jane, "let's play pirates in the attic."
"Let's not," said Dick
"We can get Mom and Dad to take us
  swimming over at Hemlock Lake," cried Jane
"No we can't," said Dick
"Oh Dick, let's invite eccentric Aunt Wilma
  and the funny old professor
  to our house for dinner;
  we always have super adventures
  when they're about,"
  cried Jane
"Let's not," said Dick
"Oh Dicky Dicky," cried Jane,
"Let's trip out into the fields
  and weave daisy garlands
  to deck our golden heads
  and pretend we're fays and elves"
"Oh for Christ's sake, Jane,"
  said Dick
  And so they didn't

Poems for Children
bp Nichol

1

This is the story of Billy Pertwilly
an ant in an anthill who did something silly.
He tried to lug back to his anthome a grape
that rolled down the slope & crushed Bill out of shape.
Now Bill's employed only for holiday brunches
coz his flat back is handy for turkeys & punches.

2

Now this is the tale of old mean Gene the shark
whose bite was definitely worse than his bark.
He tried to bite off the Great Barrier Reef
(because he felt angry) and lost all his teeth.
Now he's forced to drink soup & eat jelly for dinner
coz you can't fill your belly by gumming a swimmer.

3

High up in the rockies lived Wild Bill the goat
quite famous for bleating Shakespearian quotes.
Sure-footed, usually, he fell down one day
while acting out scenes from a well-known play.
But was Bill worried? No! He smiled as he fell
baa-ing out knowingly, "All's well that ends well."

The Sitter and the Butter
and the Better Batter Fritter
Dennis Lee

My little sister's sitter
Got a cutter from the baker,
And she baked a little fritter
From a pat of bitter butter.
First she bought a butter beater
Just to beat the butter better,
And she beat the bit of butter
    With the beater that she bought.

Then she cut the bit of butter
With the little butter cutter,
And she baked the beaten butter
In a beaten butter baker.
But the butter was too bitter
And she couldn't eat the fritter
So she set it by the cutter
    And the beater that she bought.

And I guess it must have taught her
Not to use such bitter butter,
For she bought a bit of batter
That was sweeter than the butter.
And she cut the sweeter batter
With the cutter, and she beat her
Sweeter batter with a sweeter batter
    Beater that she bought.

Then she baked a batter fritter
That was better than the butter
And she ate the better batter fritter
    Just like that.

But while the better batter
Fritter sat inside the sitter —
Why, the little bitter fritter
Made of bitter butter bit her,
Bit my little sister's sitter
    Till she simply disappeared.

Then my sister came to meet her
But she couldn't see the sitter —
She just saw the bitter butter
Fritter that had gone and et her;
So she ate the butter fritter
     With a teaspoonful of jam.

Now my sister has a bitter
Butter fritter sitting in her,
And a sitter in the bitter
Butter fritter, since it ate her,
And a better batter fritter
Sitting in the silly sitter
In the bitter butter fritter
        Sitting in my sister's tum.

Koonohple
for Myrna Kostash
Andrew Suknaski

mother enjoying some tea
and remembering how they grew koonohple back in galicia
tells of baba karasinski planting the precious round seeds
in the spring
and how she later coddled the young green leaves
the male and female plants growing side by side
from a single seed
baba wanting only the best always weeded out the male
so the female could grow tall and strong
there was never any difficulty telling them apart
though the male plants grew first
the females always flourished taller in the end
"why bother with the runts" baba must have thought
"they're only like some dido ... an obedient shadow of baba"
she probably assumed that in one's garden at least
things could be perfect
and anyway it was the female who bore all the seeds
she could survive alone

when the crop was ready
baba and dido would harvest it with sickles
and tie small bundles
later buried in a muddy trench near a creek
where they were left to rot for one week before being dug up
and taken to the creek to rinse
finally koonohple were hung on a fence to dry
and a few days later dido battered them with a flail
till only the strong hemp thread within the stalks remained
then baba's final delicate work began
using a huge piece of circular wood with many spikes
she would comb and comb the threads
until they became almost as fine as gossamer
then on winter nights baba and other women
got together with their bundles of combed koonohple
to tell stories while they spun by hand
every bundle into fine thread wound onto big wooden spools
they called "vahrahtmoos"
and mother says
their arms and hands were their spinning wheels
the thread was dyed with beet plum or carrot juice
and woven into cloth becoming
table cloths towels curtains
and clothes for a whole family

fascinated i ask mother
"what did you do with the seeds leaves and stems
after you flailed koonohple?"
mother sipping her sweet tea slowly remembers
"oh ... vee kept seeds fhorr nex yearr
an throw strrah to dha peegz ...
dhey vaz shure like dhat sthoff"
i ask if she grew koonohple on the farm
she smiles
"shomtimes ... ohnly leedly bit fhorr burds
i gif dhem seeds in veenterr
oh dhey shurr like dhem ... sing soh nice"
she tells how in the old country
dido used to press oil from koonohple seeds
and she wistfully recalls how good it was on salads
a bit of chopped homegrown onion and sliced cucumber
a tad of pepper and salt

"smell soh ghoot ... dhat oil
vit leedly veenyeegerr
nhoting else now *soh* ghood"

smiling i ask mother
"you know what koonohple are mom?"
as she eyes me suspiciously
i tell her
"grass mom 'trahvah' that's the stuff the kids smoke mom"
she lifts her braided fingers high above her head
rolls her eyes heavenward
and exclaims
"oooh my God ... maryyohnah! dhat's be marryyohnah?"

and now that i mention to mother
how the kids often grow their own hiding it with corn stalks
she slowly remembers how her father
grew his illegal tobacco at the turn of the century
and hid it at the centre of his koonohple crop
that always grew taller all around
she remembers that when the first world war came
tobacco was scarce everywhere in the old country
and didos suffering withdrawal beat their babas
the old women scuttling to neighbours everywhere
to beg for a bit of tobacco
didos tried bulrushes and nettles and simply anything
and mother recalls how her grandfather silent as granite
in his corner of the living room
was often lost in a cloud of rising smoke
like a chimney on a cold windless winter morning
baba coughing and chiding dido
"dgeetko ... vahryatstvo!
ahbeh tehbeh shlock trahfogh!"
dido always mumbling between well spaced blissful eternities
and keeping his secret
"fynoo baba ... fynoo ... fchoh budeh yak zohlotoh
'beautiful old woman
beautiful ... everything will be like gold'"

Brevity is the Soul of Wit

from *Power Politics*
Margaret Atwood

you fit into me
like a hook into an eye

a fish hook
an open eye

Epigram
Joseph Howe

[On *being told by a Lady that the face was an index to the mind.*]

Although you protest it again and again,
   I still must believe you are jesting,
For what must thy exquisite volume contain
   When the Index is so interesting?

World's Shortest Pessimistic Poem
Robert Zend

Hope?

Nope.

Truce
P. K. Page

My enemy in a purple hat
looks suddenly like a plum
and I am dumb with wonder
at the thought
of feuding with a fruit.

Party Time
Louis Dudek

"Desirable bodies. There are so many . . . "
Nature's box of candy —
                    "Take one please."

Sometime later, if you're lucky:
"Have another?"

And the desire lingers, between invitations,
like pepperpot pastrami on the tongue.

Live it up, Chiquita.

Lyrique d'Amour Propre
Robert Allen

i think you are nicer
than Theodore Dreiser

Poem
Leonard Cohen

the 15-year-old girls
I wanted when I was 15
I have them now
it is very pleasant
it is never too late
I advise you all
to become rich and famous

The Bourgeois Child
Raymond Souster

I might have been a slum child,
I might have learned to swear and steal,
I might have learned to drink and whore,

but I was raised a good bourgeois child,
and so it has taken me a little longer.

News Item Oct. 10/69
Don Bailey

krupp corp. announces plans
to manufacture military equipment
but assure us:

"we do not make any military item
that goes bang."

oh goody, goody
quiet wars.

The Use of Force
John K. Rooke

Please don't believe
The use of force
Is how we change the social course;
The use of force
You surely know
Is how we keep the status quo.

poemsoup

mary howes

carrot
onion
turnip and
green

calliope   bayou   cadence   serene

barley
bayleaf
potato and
leek

ephemeral   cygnet   etude   lalique

zucchini
tomato
pepper and
corn

chimerical   bodkin   calyx   forlorn

Poem Composed in Rogue River Park, Grant's Pass, Oregon After Wayman's Car Stopped Dead on the Oregon Coast in the Middle of a Howling Rainstorm and Had to Be Towed First to Yachats, Oregon, Where It Couldn't Be Fixed and Then One Hundred Miles Through the Mountains to Eugene, Where After It Was Repaired and Wayman Started Out Again His Accelerator Cable Parted and He had to Run on the Last Dozen Miles or So into Grant's Pass at Midnight with His Throttle Jammed Open and Spend the Night Waiting for the Garage to Open Which Is at this Moment Working on His Car, or Rather Waiting for a New Part to Be Shipped Down from Eugene (and Which Garage, Incidentally, Would Fix the Cable but Fail to Discover that All that High-Rev Running Would Have Blown the Head Gasket on Wayman's Car Causing Frightening Over-Heating Problems the Next Day When Wayman Did Try to Blast on down to San Francisco)
Tom Wayman

Let me not go anywhere.
Let me stay in Grants Pass, Oregon, forever.

Martinigram
F. R. *Scott*

The key person in the whole business
I said raising my Martini damn that woman
she didn't look where she was going sorry
it won't stain the key person what? oh it's
you Georgina no I won't be there tomorrow
see you some day the key person in the whole
business is not the one oh hello James yes
we're having a wonderful time not the one you
love but it's no thank you no more just now
not the one you love but it's the one who
does the hell's bells there's a stone in my olive

The Artist's Lot
Al Pittman

When we meet
he tells me
that I am
his wife's favourite poet

In a minute
he will tell me
what a stupid woman
his wife happens to be

Press
Bruce Bentz

The large white porcelain button
in the middle of the ceiling
either
rings the building
or ejects the roof

Vaughan's World
Francis Sparshott

I saw eternity the other day
Most like a ring of drab unending grey.
"Look! there's eternity!" said my mother-in-law.
"Yes, Mother," said my wife. "We know. We saw."

First Lesson in Theology
Alden Nowlan

"God is a Baptist,"
my grandmother told me
when I was three.
"John the Baptist baptized him,
so what else could he be?"

Roman Numeral
Francis Sparshott

When Housman came to Ludlow
he brought his writing-pads;
his heart was full to bursting
for all those Shropshire lads.

Some died upon the gallows
while Housman wrote and cried,
and some in bars or battles;
but, anyway, they died.

Night falls on Ludlow churchyard
where Housman lies alone,
and Shropshire dogs come creeping
to piss against the stone.

A Little Black Poem
Jon Whyte

Little Jerry quite contrary
memorized a dictionary.
It didn't help in any way —
Jerry had no thing to say.

The Birds & the Beasts

Position of Sheep 1
Steve McCaffery

                                   sheep

                                          sheep

                                            sheep

                 sheep
          sheep   lamb

                                      sheep

     sheep

                                      sheep

7.21 PM
8.v.78

Royal Cowflap

David Berry

We came upon it
after endless corridors.

"This is from the Royal Cow,"
said the tower guard
and nudged it
with the toe of his boot.

"It's only slightly smaller
than that said to have been passed
by the legendary Minotaur
of ancient Greece,"

he added, quoting
Facts About the Royal Keep.

"It's a piece of shit," said Mrs. Harwood-
Barker, and resolutely held
her handkerchief to her nose.

Horse
Sarah Binks

Horse, I would conjecture
Thoughts that spring in thee:
Do, in contemplative hour,
Teeming doubts thy soul devour,
As in me?
Does some yeasty cranial power,
Intellectual force,
Urge, in kindred doubts that grip us;
"I, who once was eohippus,
Now am horse;
I have thinking,
Therefore being,
Therefore smelling,
Feeling,
Seeing;
Therefore horse.
Gloriously horse!
Horse I am but would be gladder
Could I see,
Evolutionary ladder's
Certainty;
Horse I am but can I know,
With the loss of final toe,
What to be?
Nought there is to tell me if
Pegasus or Hippogriff
Is destiny.
Oh well,
Horse's heaven,
Horse's hell,
Or super-horse,
Who can tell?
Who denotes?
What with knowledge and reflexes,
Self-expression and complexes,
Inhibitions and the sexes —
Give me oats.

The Elephant Dream
Anne Szumigalski

the elephant dream is for spring
when we paint the outside of the house
you go downtown to buy a ladder
but instead you purchase
a rather old sway-backed elephant

the elephant stands quietly under the dormer windows
you stand on its broad back
carefully painting the window frames
a gallon of white paint
is balanced on the animal's head

when it is my turn to paint,
the elephant, in spite of its size,
objects to my sturdy weight
it lopes away across the prairie
with me clinging to its ears
it rears and screams horribly
white paint pours down one side of its trunk

you bravely give chase
and skilfully capture the beast
lock it in the small back porch of our house

the elephant breaks the windows
scattering glass into the flowerbeds
then, after a whole minute of silence
we hear the terrible pouring
it is pissing out its huge elephant bladder
the floor is knee-deep in urine
we can hear the elephant sloshing about inside
trumpeting its triumph

meanwhile we stand about in the yard
watching ragged puffs of honey-smelling steam
escape through the broken panes

Beaver
David McFadden

She was writing a story on the beaver
for *ForesTalk*
the magazine of the B.C. ministry of forests
and she could talk of nothing else
as we sat together on the bus
her eyes were all fevered
with talk of the beaver.

I'd heard it all before
how the beaver was originally the "beofor"
and is descended from the 700-pound beast
that inhabited Europe and the east
a million years ago or more.

Then suddenly she looked into my eyes and cried
"The beaver does a much better job
of dam building than man, and much cheaper."

"That certainly is a marvellous thing"
I said, wanting to be kind in my boredom
but suddenly my boredom disappeared
when she told me how she'd been sunbathing
near the beaver dam she'd been inspecting
and dozed off and was slowly awakened
by a giant beaver who had mounted her!
"The beaver does a much better job of other things
than man as well" she said with a sexual smile

and before I could figure out what to say
she said "Oh, here's my stop. Good day!"

For Greg Corso
Glenn Deer

      dear greg
        my new rabbitz hate poetry   i keep
   tellin em and tellin em words is fun but they
 refuse to read it   i tell em they're lazy and
    they start cryin and makin messy poo poos
on the carpet.
            when they're not sleepin or watchin
 the bugs bunny road runner hour they sing
gregorian chants or play morbid frank sinatra records
     until i scream at em   its hard puttin up with it
  all they wanna eat are carrots and when i took em
to Boston Pizza they bit the waitress on the buttocks
      cause they thought she called em a bunch of
bum bunnies when she really said dumb bunnies and
        they deserved it cause they were sharpening
 their teeth on the metal edges of the jukebox   anyways
   i told em and it worked like a miracle
  shape up or ship out i says and now gosh
they're both takin automotives courses at nait and
             drivin taxis part time   they're finally
      growin up

Four Skinny Pigs Make Two Head-Cheeses
Michael Harris

Once I raised four skinny pigs;
The best was Esmerelda.
The other three were Parsley Sprigs,
Slim-as-a-Nail and Zelda.

Young Parsley Sprigs was almost green;
Slim-as-a-Nail was bony.
And Zelda's mien was dark and lean:
Tough as a coal-mine pony.

Sweet Esmerelda took the prize:
None of those pigs could touch her;
I had to tell her raging lies
To have her meet the butcher.

Then Slim and Zelda ran zags and zigs,
Turned pale and downright skittish;
And Parsley Sprigs did Irish jigs
But the butcher's knife was British.

They went the way all piggies do,
Except in smaller pieces;
Combined, they might have stocked a stew,
Made two, not four, head-cheeses.

The Strange Case
Michael Ondaatje

My dog's assumed my alter ego.
Has taken over — walks the house
phallus hanging wealthy and raw
in front of guests, nuzzling
head up skirts
while I direct my mandarin mood.

Last week driving the baby sitter home.
She, unaware dog sat in the dark back seat,
talked on about the kids' behaviour.
On Huron Street the dog leaned forward
and licked her ear.
The car going 40 miles an hour
she seemed more amazed
at my driving ability
than my indiscretion.

It was only the dog I said.
Oh she said.
Me interpreting her reply all the way home.

Noctambule

George Johnston

Mr Murple's got a dog that's long
And underslung and sort of pointed wrong;
When daylight fades and evening lights come out
He takes him round the neighbour lawns about
To ease himself and leak against the trees
The which he does in drops and by degrees
Leaving his hoarded fluid only where
Three-legged ceremonious hairy care
Has been before and made a solemn sign.
Mythology, inscrutable, canine,
Makes his noctambulation eloquent
And gives a power of meaning to his scent
That all who come and sniff and add thereto
And scratch the turf, may know they have to do
With Mr Murple's underslung long dog,
His mark, his manifesto and his log.

Mr. Scales Walks His Dog

Alexander Hutchison

The dog is so old dust flies out from its arse as it runs;
the dog is so old its tongue rattles in its mouth, its eyes were changed
in the 17th century, its legs are borrowed from a Louis Fourteen
bedside cabinet.
The dog is barking with an antique excitement.
Scales dog is so old its barks hang in the air like old socks,
like faded paper flowers.
It is so old it played the doorman of the Atlantic Hotel in *The Last Laugh*,
so old it played the washroom attendant too.
Scales dog is so old he never learned to grow old gracefully.
Scales dog bites in stages.
Scales dog smells of naphtha.
Scales dog misjudges steps and trips.
Scales dog begs for scraps, licks plates.
Scales dog is seven times older than you think:
so he runs elliptically; so he cannot see spiders; so he is often distracted;
so he loses peanuts dropped at his feet; so he has suddenly become diabetic
and drinks from puddles; so there is bad wind in his system that came over
with the Mayflower; so he rolls on his back only once a week.
Scales dog is Gormenghast, is Nanny Slagg.
Scales dog is Horus, is Solomon Grundy.
His body makes disconnected music.
He is so old his eyes are glazed with blood;
so old wonders have ceased; so old all his diseases are benign; so old he
disappoints instantly; so old his aim is bad.
Scales dog is so old each day Scales urges him to die.
Scales dog puts on a show like a bad magician.
Scales dog squats as if he was signing the Declaration of Independence.
Scales dog is so old worms tired of him.
So old his fleas have won prizes for longevity.
So old his dreams are on microfilm in the Museum of Modern Art.
So old he looks accusingly.
So old he scratches for fun.
Scales dog was buried with the Pharaohs, with the Aztecs; draws social
security from fourteen countries; travels with his blanket; throws up on
the rug; has a galaxy named after him; Scales dog runs scared;
would have each day the same, the same;
twitches in his sleep,
wheezes.

The Publican's Dog
Kevin Roberts

that dog there, Samson, he says
ruddy face mutton chops
mine host of the Stowey Arms
voice slurred
with centuries of cider and cream
be as fierce an animal
as you could hope to meet

and I turned to look at the beast
lying where it always did
like an overstuffed cushion
by the gas fire on the carpet
in the Bar
munching a string of snags
in a slow mournful way
so fat it could hardly
lift its heavy chops to lick them
ponderous body shag brown and white
a beagle so obese
its stubs of legs
could hardly support it
walked slow as a turtle
remembering the strange sight
even for England
of the publican walking his dog
its belly and ears
trailing in the mud
wheezing behind its master
fierce as a fairy-tale dragon
mine host in deerstalker cap
and shooting stick
taking the air across the fields
behind the pub
but beloved of the publican
who cared not for his neighbours
who in turn detested this beast
which left huge ribbons of dog shit
resembling rock pythons at bay
in their gardens

booby traps for those
who attacked them
at close quarters
with hoe or spade

noticing today over a Sunday pint
something different about
the immobile beast
lying even more thickly
spread on the carpet
tiny legs swathed in bandages
collapsed at right angles
to its bulk

and mine Host
noticing my glance says
deep admiration in his voice
brave dog that
blind reckless you might say
last night we had an intruder
and he paused for the horror of it
to sink into the Bar

and Samson there
in hot pursuit
leaped off our front step
in one great bound
broke all his legs
brave chap
in defence of this house

and we turned as one to
look in disbelief
at the 4 inch step
at the front door
and at this huge dog
peering sublimely down its nose
its heroism painfully clear.

Postcard from Picadilly Street
Michael Ondaatje

Dogs are the unheralded voyeurs of this world.
When we make love
the spaniel shudders
walks out of the room,
she's had her fill of children now

but the bassett — for whom
we've pretty soon got to find a love object
apart from furniture or visitors' legs —
jumps on the bed and watches.

It is a catching habit having a spectator
and appeals to the actor in both of us,
in spite of irate phone calls from the SPCA
who claim we are corrupting minors
(the dog being one and a half).

We have moved to elaborate audiences now.
At midnight we open the curtains
turn out the light
and imagine the tree outside
full of sparrows
with infra red eyes.

Birdwatching at the Equator
Al Purdy

The blue-footed booby
stands on her tropic island
in the Galapagos group
stands all day long
shading her eggs from the sun
also protecting her blue feet
from too much ultraviolet

Sometimes the male booby
flaps his wings and dances
to entertain his mate
pointing his toes upward
so they can discuss blueness
which seems to them very beautiful
Their only real enemy
is the piratical frigate bird
floating on great black wings
above the mile-long island
Sometimes the frigate bird
robs them of their fish
whereupon the booby
is wont to say "Friggit"
and catches some more
When night comes all the boobies
sit down at once as if
God had given them a signal
or else one booby says
to the rest "Let's flop boys"
and they do

The blue booby's own capsule-
comment about evolution:
if God won't do it for you
do it yourself:
stand up
sit down
make love
have some babies
catch fish
dance sometimes
admire your feet
friggit:
what else is there?

Galapagos Islands

Herons
Robert Fones

I saw a heron today.
I didn't see *The Heron*.
That's him in the bird book
he looked just like that.
But did you see that heron?
No, it was another heron — Nobody
could see *that* heron.
Then you didn't see that heron. No, but
I did see a heron.

Have you ever seen herons on Lake Huron?
Not around here.
Not around here isn't anywhere near Lake Huron. Isn't
anywhere near Lake Huron? Somewhere is
but they don't see herons there.
At least, not these herons.

I've seen herons here and there
but usually thunder.
Usually I hear thunder and then I see a heron. Once
I saw a heron standing in exactly the same spot
where I'd seen another heron.
But it wasn't the same heron. I hear
herons are hard to see.
Not at all if you look in exactly the same spot
where I see herons all the time.
I usually do
but I only hear thunder.

Point Pelee, June 1977

The Fox and the Stick
Bill Howell

1.
"That was mid-summer, smack
in the middle of flea season,
and he spent most of the morning
scratching like crazy
while I watched.
                    And while I watched,
he took a foot long stick in his mouth
and headed straight for the lake.

"Where slow and deliberate, he
lowered himself into the water,
backwards so those fleas hopped
further and further up his back
to his head to keep high and dry.

"And he left them all behind there,
floating on that stick like a bunch
of shipwrecked sailors seen through
the wrong end of a telescope.
                    And he swam
a good twenty feet underwater.

"Before he came out drenched
while I watched him, and I swear
he shook himself off with a grin."

2.
"One afternoon, late last fall,
I was driving home when I spotted him
trotting across the lake ice.

"Stopped the truck, and took out
the binoculars, wondering what
the hell's he doing out there
this time of day?
                    And crazy bastard,
what's he got that stick there
in his mouth again for?

"Checked out the whole lake, and sure
enough, there was a bunch of mallards
swimming around in an open spot, about
a hundred yards off his shoulder.

"But he just ignored them, started
playing around with his stick,
tossing it up in the air and rolling
around on his belly like some
stupid puppy, while the ducks
craned and tilted their heads and necks
to watch.

"And sure as hell, first one and then
the whole bunch of those ducks
crawled out and started shoving each
other across the ice towards him, like
they were hypnotized or something,
they all wanted to sit ringside.

"And he was cucumber cool, kept on
frigging around with his stick
and not looking like he was looking
until they were almost right up to him,
waddling across the ice there.

"And then he nailed the biggest one
so quick it took my breath away."

How Mice Make Love
Joe Rosenblatt

How mice make love
is none of your business
but for a peeping poet
the micelings are intolerant
of lurid human observation.

The sky cold eye is magnified
telescoping musical midgets
scampering in beds of tiny love;
in a twilight of burning candles
mini-mammals throw mini-shadows.

No mouse has read the Kama Sutra
they never take reading material to bed
what do they care about
HUMAN SEXUAL RESPONSES?
In love, mice make out gloriously
their teeny weeny fingers seem
more velvet than Aphrodite's paws
when fluid midnight moons light up
a little lachry mouse's love.

Eurynome
Jay Macpherson

Come all old maids that are squeamish
And afraid to make mistakes,
Don't clutter your lives up with boyfriends:
The nicest girls marry snakes.

If you don't mind slime on your pillow
And caresses as gliding as ice
— Cold skin, warm heart, remember,
And besides, they keep down the mice —

If you're really serious-minded,
It's the best advice you can take:
No rumpling, no sweating, no nonsense,
Oh who would not sleep with a snake?

Giraffes Are All Right
Suniti Namjoshi

One day a whole herd of giraffes
                    entered my bedroom.
I was greatly enamoured.
                    Their mouths were tender
and their coats dappled.
                  Their sex burgeoned
like a double flower.
                  But giraffes, you understand,
are quite all right:
                  their stylized necks
and thin limbs
                  makes it easy to see them
as objects of art.

London, June 3, 1978
Miriam Mandel

I walked
down
Cromwell Road today
under
a setting sun
to look
at
the fishes and bugs
in the Museum of Natural History.
The only thing
I saw
there
that seemed buggy
was me.
The eels merely eely, slime
lizards, rough and scaly,
some fishes appeared appetizing —
but, particularly, the bugs
seemed
in control
antennae listening
not waving wildly
in any self-induced wind.
I am, by far and away,
the oddest thing
I saw today
at the
Museum of Natural History.

Love's Humours

In Defence of Free Lust
Helene Rosenthal

I sat upon a satyr & satirical was I
for I had a little faun beside
a little faun had I
O nymph, O mania they shrieked
as we pranced wildly by

I lay with Love & did him prove
a loving lay sang I
& hill & valley dale & field
did yield to see us lie

Come live with me & be my guest
& I'll not let thee down
for up thou always will be best
& I up with my gown

A thing of joy is goat or boy
or maiden paired with maiden
Then let us feast us while we may
though fruit trees be forbidden

O back us Bacchus with thy reign
& never do hold back
for wine will sour to vinegar
for those who practise lack

For Beauty is a rime forever
Rarely do the poets lie
who hate the prose of abstinence
and so do I

Poem Improvised Around a First Line*
Gwendolyn MacEwen

the smoke in my bedroom which is always burning
worsens you, motorcycle Icarus;
you are black and leathery and lean and
you cannot distinguish between sex and nicotine

anytime, it's all one thing for you —
cigarette, phallus, sacrificial fire —
all part of that grimy flight
on wings axlegreased from Toronto to Buffalo
for the secret beer over the border —

now I long to see you fullblown and black
over Niagara, your bike burning and in full flame
and twisting and pivoting over Niagara
and falling finally into Niagara,
and tourists coming to see your black leather wings
hiss and swirl in the steaming current —

now I long to give up cigarettes
and change the sheets on my carboniferous bed;
O baby, what Hell to be Greek in this country —
without wings, but burning anyway

* The first line around which it was improvised has disappeared.

East-North-East
Craig Powell

An erection I've had nine
days now won't go down   a
rigged bowsprit under full sail
it cruises the cultured bays of
our suburb   I float behind
embarrassed   I'd rather it weren't
mine   I try to hide it

by stuffing towels in
my trousers   but the school-
girls still gawp
and giggle and the lady
in the supermarket is disgusted
but keeps flicking her tongue   I
don't even know how
it got to be there   it just
snapped up   blew out its
spinnaker and hauled
me down wind at   believe me   a
frightening pace   it's these lacquered
curious fingers that really
make me sweat and I try
to keep my back turned to the police
cruiser   the newspaper
boy smiles softly and asks
me my phone number   that's
the trouble!   they
all think it's for them!   even
my wife who I'd hoped
would be more understanding
is saying Enough Is Enough
and Is There Someone Else
Dear?   this isn't really
happening   nine days
aloft and adrift I
heel down the foaming shoals
of pizza parlours   bank
lobbies   boutiques of lubricious
matrons   buses agog with flash-
bulb-eyed and yelping kids   the
old pirate in charge at last

obedience training
mary howes

you come into me from behind
good
i can't see anything this way
it could be
a wand
a bone
here rover
lie down
roll over
play dead

Leda in Stratford, Ont.
Anne Wilkinson

A silly country maiden went
A mile or so to Stratford, Ont.,
And here she found, as everywhere,
Things much too ordin'ry for her;
Yet from a Richard, Rex, or clown
She learned of Leda and the Swan,
And so admired their high-class union
That up and down the banks of Avon
She ogled those immaculate birds
That never turned to take her crumb
Or listen to her honeyed words
Of love, but simply swam.

A crow, observing her odd wish,
Laid the girl beneath a bush;
No sudden blow — the great wings beating —
More as a joke, a kind of larking.
And yet she doted on his action,
Tickled by such rare seduction,
Boasting to the birds, "Black Swan,
Demon Lover urged me on."
But no bird listened, for a caw,
Loud and rude, came from the crow.

Identification Question
Robert Kroetsch

Her hair was like:

a. a field of poppies, the opium
   promise/lifting your nose

b. a carpet of red leaves, the slope
   of her long thighs/bare

c. a forest fire in the Labrador night,
   unchecked, burning

d. all of the above

*Her breasts in the throes of your
hungering love:*

a. nippled and swung like bells

b. stung your lips like irate hornets

c. swam in your sweat like mouthing
   fishes

d. hammered your chest like the beaks
   of two ravenous/doves

Her face when she came:

a. St. Teresa in the ecstasy of her
   spear-filled heart

b. the Medusa in her snaky hair, stone
   writhing

c. pieta, pieta, the mother holding
   the love of her   breaking/
   son

d. It was dark. You couldn't see. You
   weren't looking.

French Kissing

George Johnston

There is a kind of kissing they call French kissing
Which if you dont know you dont know what you're missing;
Practised by Ottawa girls it must be a snare
Men being what they are here, and girls everywhere.
Let no single Ottawa man be smug
Because he thinks he can give any girl a hug:
This leads on to the kiss and then the French kiss
And so downhill at a fearful rate to the abyss
Of diapers, runny noses, parent-teacher associations, consanguinity;
But the alternative, do not forget, is Ottawa single masculinity.

Nonstop Jetflight to Halifax

George Johnston

Never such comfort, annihilation
of the way there. But that's me! I
am the way there. These blandishments, these
knees and elbows bringing me food and drink
in high sunshine over high cloud

    to distract me.

Now that we're so far up why dont we stay?

Non-question of a non-questioner
as the stewardess knows having
smiled on my effacement.
But she gives me a look.
Never mind, I say. Sit down
beside me. Perhaps on me.

The Cuckold's Song

Leonard Cohen

If this looks like a poem
I might as well warn you at the beginning
that it's not meant to be one.
I don't want to turn anything into poetry.
I know all about her part in it
but I'm not concerned with that right now.
This is between you and me.
Personally I don't give a damn who led who on:
in fact I wonder if I give a damn at all.
But a man's got to say something.
Anyhow you fed her 5 MacEwan Ales,
took her to your room, put the right records on,
and in an hour or two it was done.
I know all about passion and honour
but unfortunately this had really nothing to do with
        either:
oh there was passion I'm only too sure
and even a little honour
but the important thing was to cuckold Leonard Cohen.
Hell, I might just as well address this to the both of you:
I haven't time to write anything else.
I've got to say my prayers.
I've got to wait by the window.
I repeat: the important thing was to cuckold Leonard
        Cohen.
I like that line because it's got my name in it.
What really makes me sick
is that everything goes on as it went before:
I'm still a sort of friend,
I'm still a sort of lover.
But not for long:
that's why I'm telling this to the two of you.
The fact is I'm turning to gold, turning to gold.
It's a long process, they say,
it happens in stages.
This is to inform you that I've already turned to clay.

Love Letter

John Newlove

How are you? And whose
hero do you want me
to be. My tooth hurts

and it is raining, there is
no oil for the stove.
Or when there is

it leaks on the floor.
Is your father well?
I'm spitting

blood again, from
that abscessed tooth
I always suck on.

And how is your father:
that bastard I've never met.
And your mother.

Goddamn them both. I hope
I never meet them. Or
you again. Love.

On the Porch

George Johnston

What's on your mind tonight,
  Mary bloody Jane?
Why do you click the light
  Laughing like a drain?
Gentlemen are a dying race,
  Click it on again!

It isn't the way you walk
  Drifting down the street,
It isn't the way you talk
  Doing things with your feet,
It isn't the way you friz your hair
  And make your odours sweet.

A fellow's not made of glass
  Nor he isn't made of steel,
Some of the time he's an ass
  Some of the time he's a heel
Some of the time he's a shot down god
  And that's the way I feel.

The Linguistic War Between Men and Women
Michael Ondaatje

                and sometimes
I think
women in novels are too
controlled by the adverb.
As they depart
a perfume of description.

"She left the table
and left her shoe
behind, *casually*"

"Let's keep our minds
clear, she said drunkenly."
The print hardly dry on
words like that.

My problem tonight
is this landscape.
Like the sanskrit lover
who sees breasts in the high clouds
testicles on the riverbed.
("The army left their balls
behind crossing into Bangalore
she said, mournfully")

Every leaf bends
I can put my hand
into various hollows, the dogs
lick their way up the ditch
swallow the scent
of whatever they eat.

Always wanted to own
a movie theatre
called "The Moonlight"

What's playing at *The Moonlight*
she asked
leafily . . .

Men never trail away.
They sweat adjective.
"She fell into
his unexpected arms."
He mixes a "devious" drink.
He spills his maddened seed
onto the lettuce...

Home-Made Beer
Al Purdy

I was justly annoyed 10 years ago
in Vancouver: making beer in a crock
under the kitchen table when this
next door youngster playing with my own
kid managed to sit down in it and
emerged with one end malted —
With excessive moderation I yodelled
at him
    "Keep your ass out of my beer!"
    and the little monster fled —
Whereupon my wife appeared from the bathroom
where she had been brooding for days
over the injustice of being a woman and
attacked me with a broom —
With commendable savoir faire I broke
the broom across my knee (it hurt too) and
then she grabbed the breadknife and made
for me with fairly obvious intentions —
I tore open my shirt and told her calmly
with bared breast and a minimum of boredom
    "Go ahead! Strike! Go ahead!"
Icicles dropped from her fiery eyes as she
snarled
    "I wouldn't want to go to jail
    for killing a thing like you!"
I could see at once that she loved me
tho it was cleverly concealed —
For the next few weeks I had to distribute
the meals she prepared among neighbouring
dogs because of the rat poison and
addressed her as Missus Borgia —
That was a long time ago and while
at the time I deplored her lack of
self control I find myself sentimental
about it now for it can never happen again —

Sept. 22, 1964: P.S., I was wrong —

A Man from France
Susan Musgrave

He's a dancer
he makes you wild

he dances the dance of
lonely women

he's a deserter.

I lived with him
he made me smile

that was enough for me
but not enough for those
French ladies.

Bitches, they were brought up
differently.

They wanted a man to marry,
a man to bury.

They didn't want Harry.

What Do You Want?

John Newlove

I want a good lover
who will not mistreat me
and suffers indignities willingly;
who is so good in bed
she covers my faults and will claim
the skill's mine, and love me,
and gossip too
to enhance my sexual fame —

what do you want,
what do you want?

I want a good lover
who will cook good meals
and listen respectfully;
shine my shoes, back my lies
with invented statistics at parties;
suffer indignities willingly
and be at my heels —

what do you want,
what do you want?

I want a good lover
who will keep her mouth shut
except for my praise to my face
or loudly behind my back;
who hates my enemies
and willingly suffers indignities —

what do you want,
what do you want?

I want a lover
who suffers indignities.

My Boots Drive Off in a Cadillac

Susan Musgrave

Always when I am dreaming
my boots, with my socks inside them,
drive off in a Cadillac
and I have to go barefoot
looking for nightlife.

The car has California plates —
I'll never forget it.
I'll never forget those boots, either.
They were handtooled in Italy.

They were always too big for me,
they slipped off easily.
I never did think they were meant for me.
They were made for someone who was
far less flighty.

The socks had a special significance,
they were given to me by a sailor.
They were a size too small but he
wanted me to wear them.
He wasn't what you'd call a sophisticated
person.

I don't know what it symbolizes,
this dream where nothing fits properly.
It's almost as if I were going around naked,
or worse, with no body at all
to make the old men wet their lips and ogle.

The men think they can buy me.
Up and down the strip I walk with a
hard line for takers; I'm no bargain.
I'm looking for a good time, a change
won't do it.
I'm dreaming of something more than a change
when my boots drive off in a Cadillac.

June Allyson

Eugene McNamara

you were always ready for bed
or in bed dreaming house
beautiful puppies twins in
their cute cribs everything
white little league perhaps
you wake up & hubby isnt on his
side of the cute bed hes in
the kitchen eyes tight over
a cigarette bent over a coffee
what to tell the goddamn boss
the org man at 4 am angst god
a closet full of picture windows
grey flannel sold out sold out

get up june get up you always
know what to do what to say
how to look when to keep quiet
when to look cute when to pout

put on the cute fluffy gown
over the white fluffy nightie
pout that lower lip like a
drop of dewy sticky gummy
candy go to the kitchen say
harry come to bed or *tom*
itll look better in the
morning or *honey ill put*
the coffee on jesus you
always knew how to look
what to say when to say it

now its time to help me
june i need your fluffy
frilly cute pouty lip
organdy bedside lamps
call me back to bed
hold me worrying about
selling out mortgages
affairs with secretaries
fascist boss cold war
suburban politics lawns
june call me *gene come*
back to bed honey dont worry

The Story of a Marrying Man

Mary Di Michele

What he really went for were women
with the clean blondeness of white wine,
squeezed from grapes shining with an oily polish,
filmed in the afternoon light.
Chilled for dinner women
wearing long fitted sleeves of plain cotton
in the full heat of summer.

He had a fondness for untested liquors
for the brew the morning made
for the evening's languor.
He had a few lazy bones
but he could make his own way
cutting hair in his own barber shop,
one chair and a Fiat 500 he drove
the half block to work.

At thirty-five he was almost ripe enough
for a little apricot of a girl
he had met in the spring.
What she always wanted was to be loved
and to get away from her mother,
what she always wanted was to watch a man soar
like a green kite snapping in a blue breeze
tied to him by the string she jiggled.

A fiance is the moon,
but a husband is its darker side,
and a bride can age into an old woman
in just twenty-eight days
while she waits for his sodden return
after nights playing cards at the cafe bar,
expecting to find her curled up for him
in freshly ironed sheets,
the chaste ribbon of her white gown
tied into a knot.
When a man gets bored with sex
it's time to marry and raise a family.

Every member of his family agreed
that he made a most excellent husband,
the burden of having his own way
suited him best,
red faced as the china bull,
souvenir from their wedding,
still burdened with the confetti:
candy coated almonds wrapped in puff balls of veil,
that wasted its seed on the vanity
into her scented talc.
He had to whistle for his wife
but never for his mother,
his mamma never needed to be told,
the thing was done
even before he could think to want it.

They all lived together by the grace of his mother
in the house her widow's pension kept
and he was the door that went walking
and the door that slammed things shut,
the chickens ran in and out freely,
ignorant of what it means to be respectable,
gossiping into the grain.

Trained by her mother-in-law
she became an acceptable wife
so when he whistled
she never barked,
she came running with her sleeves rolled up,
her hot face dusted with flour.

The natural growth of the family made her big
with babies like apples
tucked into her apron pockets.
She slipped into the role of mother she feared
with a touch of bravado
like small breasts into a padded bra.

Dishpan Hands
Monty Reid

I touch you and you're
about as warm as dishwater.
Tonight I washed them for you,
my hands in the water with
the peels and grease and
the porridge that still
clogged the drain. Of course
I expected something for it.

And now in the moonlight
that spills like rinse water
from the tap in the sky
our bodies glisten like
wet plates standing in the rack.
At least mine does. Yours
lies unscraped and filmed
with soap. You can't hear me
through the water. And when
my chapped hands reach for you
all they touch is cutlery.

Journey to Love
David McFadden

No one knows his own potential for evil
but yesterday Joan asked me to get us
a couple of Cokes

& I got a Coke for me
& a Diet-Cola for her.

"I resent this, I really resent this,"
she cried, sipping at her sweetness.

& today, forgivingly she asked
if I'd written any poems recently

& I replied yes, "but they're too deep
for you, you'd never understand them ... "

There Just Ain't No Respect
Sid Marty

"There's a vacuum cleaner
in the middle of the hall"
I whispered icily to her
breathing in the dark bed

"Is there?" she murmured huskily
Knowing damn well there was.

She'd left it there
because she's a lazy one
Only cleans the house
about once a lifetime
Not that I'm allowed to mind

But it's 4 a.m.
I had to rise to stretch my ankle
which I broke at work, on avalanche control
I tried to chop down a tree
with my ski, while my foot
was still attached
Now it throbs like mad

I got up, thinking of Jack Spicer
taking liberties with Lorca's poems
and making something other
than a simple reproduction
for english tongues

"Check that Paul's covered"
she said sleepily

It was pitch black.
I hit that vacuum cleaner
lying in the dark, like a DC 10
like a long nosed serpent
or a fireaxe with wings
in a dream of broken legs
and Lorca's poems were blown
out of my mind on a cloud of pain

There just ain't no respect for poets
in this world or the next

I cut my toe
I'm tracking blood on the hardwood floor
I don't scream, being a good husband
Just cover the child
my teeth clenched
and limp back to bed

And hissed at her
who huddled by the wall
"There's a vacuum cleaner
in the middle of the hall"

To which she answered
"whew! Your feet are cold"

I lay there, feeling like dead Lorca
executed by machinery
or in my case, a homicidal mate

Considering the folly
of dancing on my cast
while drunk, to demonstrate
the cripple's twostep

Breaking the thing in mid caper
so a nurse, white as death
must cut it off with a powersaw
and a tight smile, promising
cancer of the ankle bone

I'm wide awake
Forgotten flower
she lies in the dark,
morphine in a rose bed

I move that way.
Arms and legs engulf me
warmth dissolves me
back into sleep

Love's Humours
Susan Zimmerman

He thinks of love as a warm bath,
the water scented, softened.
He tests with a toe,
lifts in one foot, the other,
he sits — he lies —
and slides under.
Aaaah! Perfect.

His love is a warm bath
in a badly built house.
He yearns for the tap —
icy drafts prevent him.
He yearns for his robe
(marooned on a hook
halfway across the room) —
the cold floor shimmers.

Meanwhile,
the water is losing heat,
his skin shrivels and shrinks,
his weary head drops, drops
to the side —

If he thought of love
as a nourishing soup,
he'd be seated at table;
instead of perfume,
aroma of garlic, leeks,
sweet basil, green pepper;
instead of this weariness,
a comfortable hunger;
sweet carrots — delightful! —
rich tender meat,
reliable white potato.
What a safe, what a beautiful soup.
Aaaah! Perfect —
He could eat his way out.

The True Meaning of Being a Man
David Waltner-Toews

I am peeling an onion for the borscht
It is firm as a bulging bicep
I split the grainy, weather-beaten outer skin
It peels off cleanly, unequivocally
Inside: the absolute onion, colour of old ivory
smooth and sure as a man's career
Curious, I make another incision —
another layer bares itself, whiter, more vulnerable
than the last. I cut again, and again
two more shells open, delicate and lopsided
as a lover's balls
The odour of this flesh, pungent as acid
incisive as a prophet's warning
stings my nostrils
brings tears to my eyes
I become obsessed, attacking
carving my relentless way
through flesh and bone and brain
with the razor-edged calculus of a knife
each layer paler, more translucent
more precious and righteous than the last
Ruthlessly I chop them up
cast them into boiling broth
Finally, eyes gleaming
drenched in manful sweat
I have it: the tiniest of pearls
unmitigated onion, essence of cognizance
gallstone of intellect
Religiously, I lower the triumphant blade
My hands are trembling

"Aren't you putting a lot of onions in the borscht?"
my wife asks.

28/10/76
D. G. Jones

You'd think it was a single bed

I wake up with your fingers discovering
my manhood as your own

I reach behind, astonished
at my girlish bum

There's a word for us: a myth

It's not the sort of accouchement
I'd quite expected
even with the new mattress

I thought it was a simple bed

Me and You
Polly Thompson

We did it in the road and we did it in the kitchen, on the
beach, in a field; — no, that time wasn't with you, I think it
was with Danny.

And we did it in cars, in the woods and in the
yard — oh but those weren't with you, and in the canoe
was with Stan.

But in the Andes with sheep moving in and around us was
with you, and when you were the rocks and I was the
weather was with you, and the many times deep in the
Atlantic, Pacific and Arctic Oceans — in fact all the
times I remember clearly were me and you, who else, who.

Men, Snoring
Leona Gom

He could awe us all, my father,
with his barbarous snores,
that warfare in his throat
that fired his breath
in staccato volleys
across the room at us,
plundering our evenings.
"How do you sleep?" I asked my mother,
who could wake to a whisper.
"I don't hear it," she said,
which I did not believe,
and filed in memory
under Mother's Martyrdom.

My own men,
when it came my time,
I chose from their sleep,
the Silent Slumberers,
breath easing gently from them
as they lay curled on their sides;
some, I did allow
a placid dream
to bubble from their open mouths,
and later I would even tolerate
those purring gently in their sleep
like cats.

But this one, the last one —
he saws the proverbial logs
of his sleep
with a chainsaw;
his snores have loosened
plaster on the ceiling,
have homogenized the left-overs
in the refrigerator,
have shattered light bulbs
and frightened plants to death.
"How do you sleep?" asks my mother.
"Quite well," I reply.

Weather Lore
Bert Almon

Three infallible signs
that winter's here:

this morning, milk bottles
frozen in the chute

this afternoon, the door jammed
by creeping frost

tonight in bed, a woman wearing
only my woolen socks

Parental Guidance Suggested

Travelling Companions
Tom Wayman

At the bus station in Winnipeg,
buying a ticket for Winkler, Manitoba,
Wayman hears a familiar voice behind him:
"Make that two to Winkler." Wayman turns, and
it's Four Letter Word.
"I told you to stay back at the hotel,"
Wayman says. "I'll only be gone for a day.
It's a high school reading
and they asked me specifically not to bring you."
"Nonsense," Four Letter Word says,
reaching past Wayman to pay his portion of the fares.

"You're not welcome there," Wayman insists,
as he struggles out to the bus
with his suitcase and a big box of books to sell.
"That's not the point," Wayman's companion replies
as they hand their tickets to the driver
and climb up into the vehicle.
"Next you'll be ordered not to read
poems that mention smoking or drinking."

"I don't think you understand," Wayman begins
while the bus threads its way through the five o'clock traffic
and out onto the endless frozen prairie.
"The organizers of this program
asked me not to cause any trouble.
It seems somebody like you was brought into a school last year
and there were complaints all the way to the Minister of Education."

Four Letter Word stares out a window
at the darkening expanse of white snow.
"And you're the guy," he says at last,
"who's always telling people
I'm the one that gives the language its richness and vitality.
Didn't Wordsworth declare
poets should speak in the language of real men and women?"

"But it's a high school," Wayman tries to interject.
"Do you think the kids don't swear?" his friend asks.
"Or their parents? And I didn't want to bring this up,"
he continues, "but you depend on me. You use me for good reasons
and without me your performance will flop."
"No, it won't," Wayman says.
"It will," his companion asserts.
And the two ride through the deep winter night
in an unpleasant silence.

An hour later, they pull into the lights of Winkler
and here's the school librarian
waiting in the cold at the bus stop.
"You must be Wayman," he says
as Wayman steps down. "And is this a friend of yours?"
"I never saw him before in my life," Wayman responds
but his companion is already shaking hands with the librarian.
"So good to be here," he says, picking up Wayman's box of books.
"Now, when do we read?"

Disqualification
Elizabeth Brewster

I am of puritan and loyalist ancestry
and of middle-class tastes.
My father never swore in front of ladies,
as he always quaintly called women.
My mother thought that a man was no gentleman
if he smoked a cigar without asking her permission;
and she thought all men should be gentlemen,
even though a gentleman would not call himself one,
and all women should be ladies,
even though a lady would not call herself one.

I have never taken any drug
stronger than aspirin.
I have never been more than slightly drunk.
I think there are worse vices
than hypocrisy or gentility
or even than voting Conservative.

If I wanted to be fucked
I should probably choose a different word.
(Anyhow, I am not quite sure
whether it is a transitive or an intransitive verb,
because it was never given to me to parse.)

Usually I can parse words, analyse sentences,
spell, punctuate
and recognize the more common metrical forms.

It is almost impossible
that I shall ever be
a truly established poet.

Transport
Lionel Kearns

When Charley was old enough
to get his driver's licence
he bought an old Chevy sedan
and set up Betty his girl friend
in the back seat
for three dollars a crack
among his school chums
and after a while
he started to get a few
outside customers as well
and this gave him the idea
of trading the jalopy in
on a used hearse, a move
which just happened to coincide
with a new morality campaign
brought in by the City Council
the effect of which closed down
most of the existing cat houses
for some months and WOW
business boomed for Charley
to such an extent that soon
he'd got enough financial backing
to establish a city-wide fleet
of "lay-on-the-way" cars, or
to use the vulgar term
"whore-hearses," each of them
a big shiny black Caddy
with uniformed driver and
foam mattress and miniature bar
and Charley had all the cars
equipped with two-way radios
so the central office
could dispatch them to your door
within minutes of a call

At first all the action
took place at night
but after Charley switched
to another Public Relations firm
the thing really began to catch on
with business men
ordering Charley's cars
to get to luncheon appointments
or executive conferences
so they could screw away their tensions
without feeling guilty
about losing time

Eventually Charley cashed in
on the commuter market
in all the major cities
and after introducing special rates
for short inter-urban hops
he ended with a vast network
of mobile bordellos
speeding from coast to coast
across the nation
As you probably recall
Charley's letterhead
used to bear a flying ram
encircled by the motto
Come as You Go
        and Arrive Satisfied

Yes Charley played it smart
and made a pile while it lasted
because in those days
no one had thought
of legislating against, for example
"keeping a disorderly automobile"
though once Charley
got into a scrape
for having red lights
on top of his vehicles
instead of at the rear

But strangely enough
Charley's real trouble came
from the "PROFESSIONAL BROTHERHOOD
OF SMILING MORTICIANS"
who were being increasingly
plagued by people who would
flag down funeral processions
and try to climb in with the stiff
As could be expected
with that kind of opposition
the enactment of stringent
anti-sex road laws
finally put an end to the era
of the travelling orgasm
but by that time Charley
had already sold out and invested
in the munitions industry where
profits were ten times
as high, and the future
unequivocally secure

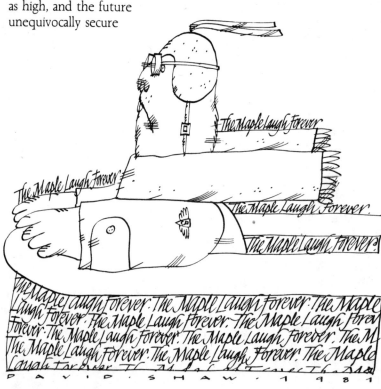

After that Charley
found himself rich enough
to slip easily into
high level politics
(I suppose it was still
the spirit of public service
which prompted him) and today
few people remember
the imagination and drive
that characterized his youth

Though I've got a hunch it was
as a kind of tribute
to Charley's remarkable background
that the Prime Minister first
made him Minister of Transport
before switching him to Defence

And incidentally I've heard it said
that even today Old Charley
shows a passing interest
in the social, as well as
the military potential
of helicopters and hovercraft

More than a Question of Taste
Elizabeth Woods

He claimed to be the renegade heir
of a respectable executive
existing on remittances and gambling
in several different ways
on horses.

Once he delivered
fourteen Thoroughbreds to Edmonton
where, without enough money to feed them
while waiting for their trainer to appear,
he sold them one by one
for foolishly low prices,
bought oats and hay
and beans for himself.

There was hell and more to pay
before the horses were properly restored
but Zeke received his fee, first
ate steak, then won the daily double.

Another time he arranged
a race, a jockey friend and he
talked the other jockeys into agreeing
how who should benefit from
who should win, but the stewards
caught wind of this conspiracy
and consequently
abandoned
       — but the heavy money from Buffalo
       already down and spoken for —

       at the end of the race
his friend fled over the backstretch fence
into Zeke's car and far away.

So you understand
that Zeke was not a timid man
except
    concerning sex
           there was one small act
           he could not perform
           cunnilingus
           or — in the vulgar tongue — eat me.

The closest he came
was one hot summer afternoon
in a bedroom of an old farmhouse
deep in the country.

Kneeling, he examined my cunt closely,
peered at me through the V of my knees,
asking: Should he? Would I mind?
I told him he should go ahead,
I liked it fine
and he said he was determined
to try
    and bravely stooped
          and almost

but, not yet,
he pulled away, laughing
at himself and his fear
and his fascination drew him
back again
        and down
                and nearly

but no
he couldn't
begin
to tell me why
he see-sawed so
intermittently
all afternoon
while we made more conventional love
and he told me stories
of horses and races.

Eventually he remembered his objective
and kneeling once more before me
leaned forward
        as far as
           he dared

but never
near enough for
the tickle of a pubic hair on his lip
like a whip sent him rearing away
eyes rolling in alarm.

In my arms I calmed him.
Finally, he said:
        I spent nine months getting out
        of there, you know
        I never was a man who liked being inside
        someone else's
        power.

At the Drive-In

Frank Davey

At the drive-in Patricia began to say
"No Edward, not yet." He would park
on a gravel sideroad on the way home
& they would embrace there beneath their clothes
& just when he was sure of what he wanted
she would say "No Edward, not yet."
He would park outside her parents' townhouse,
it would be dark & he would reach across for her
& she would say "No, not here,"
& she would open her door & run
down the paved driveway under the oak tree,
would run past the oak tree to the back porch
would run, her heels clattering on the blacktop.
& he would follow, & with her back
against the stormdoor, she would embrace him,
reach for him, & very soon
he would hear footsteps inside the house,
the back porch light would go on, & he would pull back,
but Patricia would cry out
"Now Edward, now!" & he did,
& Patricia would claw at his back
& cry "Now, now, now"
& afterward Edward would sag against the porch rail
& marvel at how the door never opened
& Patricia would say goodnight, & hurry inside,
& turn off the light.

Edward Sticks It In

Frank Davey

The baby, Patricia said,
should be born in August,
so I can go back teaching in September,
just like usual. July might do also,
she added, just to be sure
she'd acknowledged uncertainty.

So that October she went off the pill,
brought graph paper home from her school,
& bought a basal temperature thermometer
from Shopper's Drug.
We've got to do this right,
Patricia said to Edward
when November came.
You've got to leave me alone
until the right time,
to keep your sperm count up.
No wet dreams either, you sneaky bugger,
she said. Just stick the thermometer
in my mouth each morning,
she told him, & mark the temperature
on the graph. It'll stay the same
until I ovulate. Then it will go up
& the next day be way down, up & down,
like that she said, & so if you see it
go way up or way down,
you know it's time, she said.

& so Edward stuck the thermometer into Patricia's mouth
each morning, & sat hopefully on the bed.
Up & down, he thought, as the days went by.
Up & down. In & out. But at last
the thermometer moved. Patricia
checked the graph. It was up.
She lay on her back & lifted her nightie.
Edward was up Edward was in,
& Patricia said Hurry,
we'll be late for work, & Edward

was hard & long, & for the first time ever
did not come within two minutes flat,
& in fact amazed himself for five, six
seven minutes, while Patricia said
Come on, you've never had this trouble before,
& Edward was sprawled on his elbows thinking
What the hell if we are late for work,
& Patricia was saying Please,
Do something, Let's get it over with, & Edward

finally got tired of hearing this,
& pretended Patricia was a 12-year old princess
& sure to get pregnant if he came, & he did.
That evening Patricia said Let's do it again,
just to be sure, & again Edward felt
he could screw for hours,
& the next morning the thermometer was down,
& Patricia said Come on Edward, this
could be the right time too,
& that evening she said Let's make sure again,
& the following morning the thermometer was up
almost as far as before, & Patricia said
maybe this is the real one, & Edward
was not as hard as before, & that evening
not as hard as that morning, & the next morning
Patricia took his cock & stroked it
till it could enter her. It doesn't matter Edward,
she said, all you have to do
is come, she said. & so Edward
pretended she was an innocent young milk maid
& came.

"You Have Never Seen a Man Fuck a Chicken"
Artie Gold

you have never seen a man fuck a chicken
til you have seen the current pope of rome
                                    fuck a chicken.
now there is a guy
who knows what chicken-fucking's all about.
one rainy easter,
I happened to catch his act.

well there stood Giovannee
beatific in his robes
grasping
this chicken
by its giblets
and boy oh boy did that frier
drop a feather or two.
Giovannee fuckt it til the bird could no lunger cluck
til nothing clickt
til giblet gravy
made the pope's
glasses fog.

and that chicken tried so hard to please the pope
that when it died it went to heaven and still it had its
                                        wishbone intact;
so don't let them tell you
you can't take it with you
for when this bird saw god
it weren't squinting from no bucket.

The People Next Door
Eugene McNamara

i imagine them fucking all
the time shes watering those
plants in the windows he tip
toes behind her wham her skirt
is up she twists around ready
for it down they go to the cold
floor all across the rooms they
are making it no tv no kids no
dishes nothing but hard loving
wild caresses nakedness i am
jealous of all their wet joy
why do they look so dumb and
ordinary placid even when i
meet them outside oh they are
careful actors wearing bland
masks they wrench off when
the door closes in on them

Omens of Extinction are Everywhere

Genesis
Gwendolyn MacEwen

In the Beginning God was mad, and He knew it.
He took no precautions and let His mighty sperm
spill out into gorgeous space.

Stars, stars all over the place!
And all His creations were acts of madness, and
He knew it and He felt afraid.

(Monstrous moonface of the ape He made,
unholy proof of my wildest dreams.)

Some men were animals who woke up and went sane.
Moonheads. And he decided to take vengeance
on them thus:

He bestowed upon them the Black Kiss which is
the jealous kiss of God.
This He bestowed upon the loud and hungry,
on those who knew He was mad and weren't ready
to let Him get away with it. Man, He was angry
because they wouldn't let Him get away with it!

Godfather.

McGillicutty's Fundamentalism
Robert Bringhurst

True: the serpent did not always go
on his belly. There was a time when the serpent
stood up.
        Eve, like the dumb broad
that she was, said, "Hello, little serpent.
What are you doing with those little apples?"

"These?" said the serpent. "These shouldn't worry you."

Eve spoke at great length with the serpent.
In time she agreed. "That's a very nice serpent,"
said Eve.
        "Yes," said Adam.
                And Eve's
mouth grew cool like leafshade. The serpent
slinked off. Adam followed. Eve
rose up saying, "Adam! Adam! Where are you?"

Adam peered over a nearby bush.
He needed an answer. "The serpent," he said,
"led me away. I . . ."
          Eve, irate,
discerned that the serpent looked guilty. "Boys
will bruise your head, little serpent," Eve said,
"and girls will bruise your heels with their bones
and their beltbuckles."
            Adam looked on, dumbfounded,
speechless. God looked on, expressionless.

Latter Day Eve
Dorothy Livesay

But supposing (only supposing)
it was God himself, not Satan
who held up the forbidden fruit
above her vision
(and not an apple — the biblical "fruit" —
but a cluster of cherries?)
God, an old roué, lusting
held up over her head
the glowing cherries
and it was Adam
young, virile, eager
who plucked one, swiftly
and popped it into her mouth.
Ah, sweetness!
the sweetness of ripe cherry.

> When they were ushered out
> into a world of teeming traffic
> demolition deluge
> cranes screeching
> scaffolds folding
> yellow caterpillars churning up
> the lost
> the last dimension
> she glued herself to a telephone pole
> and panicked, hoarsely:
> *where are you,*
> *Adam?*
> *Adam, where are you?*

> At the motel desk
> she held up her room-key
> so he would surely
> see
> but his eyes gazed steadily past her
> at some disappearing waitress
> and she flashed the key
> fruitlessly!

Dedalus
Ronald Bates

The point is, he did not fly at all.
All those rumours about a fall
Were spread to bring me into disrepute.

A fatal accident's poor advertising.
So it's not at all surprising
To find my trade's fallen off to some extent.

But I am patient. Life and art are long
Enough to outlast rumoured wrong.
And anyway, the labyrinth's a success.

I have a name, and having that is half
The battle. I'll have the last laugh.
There's a new customer born every minute.

I'm still the fabulous artificer.
And that's a title that will wear
Better than any libellous "melted wax."

Those who know me, know me better than
To think I'd back a hare-brained plan
Like that: Man fly? What utter nonsense!

True, I've made mistakes. I'll not deny
I'm human. But to think I'd try
A stunt like that. And with my own son, too!

I stick strictly to facts, and keep my feet
Solidly on the city street.
I leave the upper air to fools and madmen.

What I make, I make for human use.
I don't believe in the abstruse
Or esoteric search for pure knowledge.

You want a fool-proof, tempered-steel lock,
A bomb set to a small clock,
A slot machine that pays a good percentange,

In fact, anything suited to practical ends?
I can supply it. And tell my friends
I'm still in business at the old address.

Dark Morning
John V. Hicks

Mother, there's a pterodactyl
perched on our aerial. He
bends it. When he folded his wings
he made the sun come out.

> Omens of extinction are
> everywhere. We don't need
> visitations of forgotten reptiles
> to twist our antennae awry.

You thought it was a dark morning.
It was his wing span, I tell you —
how many inches? No — pterodactyls
don't answer to inches.

> Hand me that duster, will you?
> Every day is a dark morning.

Here, mother. Let's not go extinct.
He's sitting there inventing feathers.

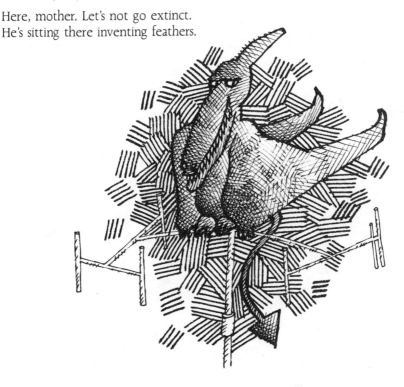

Dolores
Artie Gold

Rejected by both Rimbaud and Verlaine
she felt as bad about it as Verlaine felt about Rimbaud.
Both Verlaine and Rimbaud however felt about it only as bad as
      Rimbaud felt about Verlaine.
This is horrible thought Dolores, rejected all my life.
She felt a little like Van Gogh's ear —
the *other* one.

Rimbaud felt badly too but about other things entirely
spurned by the muse at twenty, well, maybe 18
and still / Rimbaud all his life. How/
would he live it down?

How would *she?* Well, Dolores still had a few aces up her sleeve
the ace of dildos / the ace of comfort.
She lay back yawning and rubbed herself
the year was 1888. Closing her eyes

with her penchant for pornography
she conjured up a yet unpainted "Bathers" by Cezanne.

They looked foolish in black lace garterbelts
but no more foolish than Nixon in his oval office
and only half
as naked.

Alfred Jarry Meets Emily Dickinson
David Donnell

At first he didn't know what to make of her
this prim American girl with a bun and a mouthful of teeth

Then he went to hear her read at a Boston Legion Hall
where she seemed to know only couples in their late 50's

The sort of people who appreciate someone in a sheet
who visits in the early morning and leaves poems under trees

Emily read a poem about mourning, a poem about a wedding,
a nice image of a carriage and then the poem about the fly

Alfred, sitting in the middle of the front row,
wearing as usual his stinking black suit and worn boots,

Laughed loudly at this and released a fly in the air.

Emily clutched her bodice and keeled over and died.

The audience was horrified.

The fly buzzed in the air.

Jarry laughed and caught the fly, killed it and ate it.

Walked out grinning and brushing off his filthy suit.

These Americans, he said to the doorman, they have money,
a great country, good looks; but how do they expect to meet

Angels? They have no appreciation of art and dark surprise.

Salute to Monty Python
Dorothy Livesay

What I dig is
reversals:
transvestites, almost
these 5 old ladies are
trans-generationists
who take on
the motorcycle gang
the hold-up guy
kidnappers and hi-jackers
and simply bomb the town
with the power of their ten arms.

Cheers!
to be over sixty
and running the show
with everybody scuttling
for cover.

I notice nobody
in the young audience
laughs
or is even faintly amused?
I am the only one
doubled up with mirth
(getting my own back?)

Let old age take over
with violence
ruthless possession
physical knockouts
if only to demonstrate
the other side of the mirror:
how *you* look to *us*
kiddos!

Exit Lines
George Jonas

At pesent I still have
A choice of deaths,
I could, for example, die of a difficult disease
For medical science and I could
Die for a stranger who has never learned to swim.
I could also die for the Queen.
These are quite honourable deaths
But they don't appeal to me.
I think I'll die for Barbara.
Strangers are strangers
Whether they can swim or not
Barbara is a friend.
Medical science
Requires long hours, depressing nights
In hospitals, syringes and white towels
For Barbara I could die with my clothes on.
The Queen, lovely as she is,
Has no breasts to compare with Barbara's
And I have never kissed the Queen's throat.
It makes sense for me to die for Barbara.

TH EMERGENCY WARD
bill bissett

So as i was regaining con
sciousness alone paralysd th shrink
was skreeming at me that hed never
seen such an obvious case of a
psychologically feignd man
ifestation of an apparently
physiological injury sumone
had phond in or sumthing that
i was a paintr so he sd that
again it was obvious that i was
trying by pretending
paralysis to get out of
painting that damn it

hed make me move again if he
had to shock me into it but
doctor hes bleeding nurse
shut up yu shud know
that advanced catatonia
and bleeding are not in
compatible sorry doctor
th ambulance is getting
ready so they were undr
his ordrs he kept shouting at
me bout yu and yur
kind hel fix us alright

bunduling me off to River
view th out of city mental
hospital extremely undr
staffd for shock treatment
when as they were rollin me
onto th sretchr this
beautiful neurologist chick
staff doctor sz stop thats
an inter cerebral bleed
if i ever saw one so as
th shrink had got me
first they had to
make a deal so this

is my re entry i thot so far out
so th trip was if th neurologist
chick cud get proof of an
inter cerebral bleed then i
wud go to th neurology ward
othrwise th shrinks wud get
me with inter cerebral bleed
shock treatment sure wud kill
me alright iud go out
pretty fast i gess so befor
th operation th neurologists
came to see me askd whethr i
wantid to go ahead with th
trip to the o.r. why not i
sd what have we got to

lose maybe yr life she sd well
lets get on with it alright she sd
do yu want partial total or local
iul take total evry time i sd
playd jimi hendrix water
fall thers nothing to harm yu
at all in time to th blood gushin
out of th ventricals up there to
keep them relaxd 12 neurologists
inside my brain like fantastik
voyage woke up in th middul
of th operation gave em a poetry
reading sure was fun they
put me out again sd i mustuv
known my way round drugs
cause they sure gave me a lot
well they got proof of th inter
cerebral bleed thing rescued
me from th shrinks who
still usd to sneak up th back
stairs to get at me but th nurses
usd to kick them back down
those neurologists and th nurses
in that ward sure were good
to me usd to lift th covrs off my
head which was liquifying or sum
thing my eyeballs turning to
mush ask me if there was
very much pain strong tendr
angel eyes iud say theres

so much pain don't worry we'll
bring yu anothr shot thank yu
iud moan and now i can even
write this tho th spastik fine
print in th elbow or wherever
it is is kinda strange but ium
sure lucky and grateful
fr certain that it was an intr
cerebral bleed

Unemployed Again So Desperate
David Donnell

Actually the bank of montreal needs men like me,
young, handsome, bland, and built around
spring-like coils of clearly balanced aggression.

The first bank overcomes me totally. I shove
the 5 x 7 note across the counter and stare deeply into
her eyes like a flipped hypnotist. She stiffens
and looks up at me out of her pretty face with squinted
eyes, hazel, I think, as if I were a bright figure about
a hundred yards away. "I have a gun," I tell her, and bring
the right-hand pocket of my jacket up to rest on the counter.
She nods. "All in hundreds," I tell her, "I don't want one
of those farces full of loose money stuffed in bags."

And Jesus, all I can think of as she walks across
to the cash booth, holding her head a little stiffly,
the false withdrawal slip I've given her held out in front
like a tray or something, all I can think about is what
a beautiful ass she has shifting back and forth under
her grey tweed skirt.

She comes back with the money, glancing from side to side,
adjusting the collar of her plain white shirt blouse.
"Thank you," I tell her as I pile the money neatly in my case.
"One more thing. I want you to pull your skirt up to your hips
and just stand there without saying a word. " I smile.
She stares at me in disbelief, eyes widening, mouth parting.
"Pull it up to your hips," I tell her, "right now," and I bring
my right-hand pocket up to the counter again.
She takes a deep breath and lets it out, closes her eyes
and slowly brings the grey tweed skirt up to her hips.
"Higher," I tell her, "I want to leave with you standing there."
The pulse beats in her neck and she pulls the skirt past her hips.
Pantyhose, nobody wears stockings and garters anymore, but great.

"Good," I tell her, "the gun and the sex are a little artificial
but I know the money's good." She screams and I walk out quickly,
a bland, handsome young man with a lot of aggression
and a set of car keys in his free hand. All I've ever really wanted
was to write great poems and meet beautiful and exciting women.
Paris will be like that, I tell myself getting into the stolen car.
The sun shines. And fifty bland policemen spread out somewhere
in the city to begin their usual boring search while I depart.

th tomato conspiracy aint worth a whol pome

bill bissett

very few peopul
realize ths but altho yu have 5 or 6
billyun peopul walking around beleeving

that tomatoez ar red   they ar
actually blu   nd ar sprayd
red to make ther apperance
consistent with peopuls beleef

i was whuns inside th
largest tomato spraying plant
in th world with binoculars nd
camoflage material all ovr me

nd ive got th pictures to proov it
oranges uv corz ar not orange nor ar lemons
lemon color   its all a mirage   it

was decreed what color things
wud b at th beginning nd then
theyve bin colord that
way evr since

it adds to th
chemicals nd artifishulness uv evrything
we eet tho did yu know that oranges
ar actually a discouraging off
color

i was luky really to get
out uv th tomato factoree alive
th tomatoez wer really
upset to b xposd

Supersititions
August Kleinzahler

Trout bones are taboo to dogs.
If you catch a duck
put a feather through its nostrils.
If a woman eats fresh meat
it will make her nervous;
she might even die.
It is bad luck for young people
to eat greasy fish.
If a young person steps on blood
it will make him crazy.
A menstruating woman never walks
on the beach.
If a frog comes into your house
move.

Aftermath of a Plane Wreck: Tenerife
Robert Allen

Genteel buzzards: the dentists
at Tenerife
comb the wreckage of two jumbo jets
for teeth. So badly

were the bodies disfigured: some
flimsy infrastructure, bones
and teeth,

that the puzzle is to locate
and identify the dead; and "the scale
of the tragedy,"
the papers said, required

innovative thinking. So KLM
(Royal Dutch Airlines)
ferried in its own forensic team: an entire
post-graduate course in bridgework, which

now is busy sorting
the mouths of Americans from the equally
wordless mouths of Dutch. The work

is routine, hardly a holiday in the Canaries.
Death and teeth have become
inextricably linked, making for morbid dentists,
not having a very good time. But

with ghoulish precision, they array
the darkened teeth in racks.
In the cramped lab, they are forced
to find odd places for the teeth: lab coat

pockets are full; twin
burners and briefcases are piled high;
so are the cookie jar and in/out trays
And some dentists go whimsically about

clashing the bridgework smartly, like castanets,
After all, why allow
sheer numbers of the dead
to gain death moral weight? Among

this conflagration of grins, some
Mephistopheles raises laughter: stoops
to watch the work, arranging
a trick flower

with mock fuss in
his buttonhole, says: "Are we all enjoying
our busman's holiday in Tenerife?" And
six hundred sets of teeth go *clic-cloc.*

My Latest Invention
John Steffler

I'm working on something even better than
the neutron bomb:
a device that destroys everything
but people
and plumbing.

Can't you see it!
Above the traffic and the highrise apartments
a flash, a soft
thump
people strolling the streets blink
and look around at this jungle
of monkey bars.

Folks floating in their tubs
are suddenly surrounded by nothing
but blue.

People on toilets
hundreds of feet in the air
sit tight
and stare across at one another
like astonished robins.

The bulky dross of building material
has vanished
revealing the undreamt of beauty
of the plumber's art:
breath-taking trees of naked pipes
soaring and branching to bathtubs
toilets, sinks and urinals
all hanging in the air
like porcelain fruit.

Alexander Calder's heart would burst!

Of course there *will* be casualties.
A lot of people will fall.

Only those at ground level
or on the john or in the tub
and maybe a few who are shaving or brushing their teeth
and manage to grab the sink
when the floor disappears
will be saved.

But then, no weapon is perfect
and my plumbing bomb at least
has the advantage of favouring
clean people.

Acknowledgements

The editors and the publisher wish to extend grateful acknowledgement to the following for the use of material quoted. Every effort has been made to contact copyright owners. In the case of any errors or omissions, the publisher would be grateful for any information enabling suitable acknowledgements to be made in future editions.

Milton Acorn for "In Addition" from I've Tasted My Blood, 1978, Steel Rail Publishing.
Robert Allen for "Lyrique d'Amour Propre" and "Aftermath of a Plane Wreck: Tenerife."
Don Bailey for "News Item Oct. 10/69."
Ronald Bates for "Dedalus" from The Wandering World, 1959, Macmillan of Canada.
William Bauer for "The Terrible Word," "What I Shudda Said . . ." and "The Long Summer Afternoon" from The Terrible Word, 1978, Fiddlehead Poetry Books.
Bruce Bentz for "Press."
David Berry for "Royal Cowflap" from Pocket Pool, 1975 Peppermint Press.
bill bissett for "th tomato conspiracy aint worth a whol pome" and "TH EMERGENCY WARD" from Beyond Even Faithful Legends, 1980, Talonbooks.
George Bowering for "A Poem for High School Anthologies."
Robert Bringhurst for "McGillicutty's Fundamentalism" from The Life and Times of McGillicutty: Six Arias for Tuba and Sounding Brass, not yet published.
Chickadee magazine, The Young Naturalist Foundation, for "Mean Gene the Shark" by bp Nichol.
Clarke, Irwin and Company Limited for "Disqualification" from In Search of Eros, 1974, and "The Future of Poetry in Canada" from Sunrise North, 1972, by Elizabeth Brewster.
John Robert Colombo for "A Canadian Is Somebody Who" from Variable Cloudiness, 1977, Hounslow Press.
Frank Davey for "At the Drive-In" and "Edward Sticks It In."
Glenn Deer for "For Greg Corso."
Mary Di Michele for "The Story of a Marrying Man."
David Donnell for "Alfred Jarry Meets Emily Dickinson," "How to Become a Fashionable Writer," "Rutabagas," and "Unemployed Again So Desperate."
Louis Dudek for "Party Time" and "Poetry for Intellectuals."
R. G. Everson for "The Throwback Voice" and "Greeks Had Nothing Else to Do."
Robert Fones for "Herons."
Raymond Fraser for "Canadian Poem."
Gerry Gilbert for "Calgary poems is."
Artie Gold for "You Have Never Seen a Man Fuck a Chicken" and "Dolores," and for "In the Supermarket" by Ken Norris.

Ralph Gustafson for "Irving Layton."

Michael Harris for "Four Skinny Pigs Make Two Head-Cheeses."

House of Anansi Press for "You fit into me" from *Power Politics*, 1971, by Margaret Atwood.

Bill Howell for "The Fox and the Stick."

mary howes for "poemsoup" and "obedience training."

Alexander Hutchison for "Mr. Scales Walks His Dog" from *Deep-Tap Tree*, 1978, University of Massachusetts Press.

George Johnston for "On the Porch," "French Kissing," "Nonstop Jetflight to Halifax," and "Noctambule" from *Happy Enough*, 1972, Oxford University Press.

George Jonas for "Exit Lines."

D. G. Jones for "28/10/76."

Lionel Kearns for "Negotiating a New Canadian Constitution" and "Transport" from *By the Light of the Silvery McLune*, 1969, Talonbooks.

Roy Kiyooka for "Dear Susan" from *Transcanadaletters*, 1975, Talonbooks.

August Kleinzahler for "Supersititions" from *A Calendar of Airs*, 1978, Coach House Press.

Joy Kogawa for "On Meeting the Clergy of the Holy Catholic Church in Osaka."

Robert Kroetsch for "Identification Question" and "The Silent Poet at Intermission."

Dorothy Livesay for "Salute to Monty Python" and "Latter Day Eve."

Douglas Lochhead for "Today I am thirty-nine."

Macmillan of Canada, a Division of Gage Publishing Limited, for "The Sitter and the Butter and the Better Batter Fritter" and "William Lyon Mackenzie King" from *Alligator Pie*, 1974, by Dennis Lee; for "Genesis" and "Poem Improvised Around a First Line" from *Magic Animals; Selected Poems*, 1974, by Gwendolyn MacEwen; for "The Use of Force" by John V. Rooke and "A Sovereign Nation" by Joe Wallace, from *The Blasted Pine*, 1967; for "Routines" from *Money and Rain*, 1975, by Tom Wayman.

Jay Macpherson for "Poets and Muses."

Eli Mandel for "First Political Speech."

Miriam Mandel for "London, June 3, 1978."

Steve McCaffery for "Position of Sheep 1."

The Canadian Publishers, McClelland and Stewart Limited, for "Strine Authors Meet," "Them Able Leave Her Ever," "Charité, Espérance et Foi" from *Rag and Bone Shop*, 1971, by Earle Birney; for "The Cuckold's Song" and "Destiny" from *Selected Poems*, 1968, and "Poem" from *The Energy of Slaves*, 1972, by Leonard Cohen; for "Thoughts on Calling My Next Book 'Bravo Layton '" from *The Covenant*, 1977, by Irving Layton; for "There Just Ain't No Respect" from *Nobody Danced with Miss Rodeo*, 1981; by Sid Marty; for "Beaver" and "Border Skirmish" from *On the Road Again*, 1978, and for "A True Poem" from *Intense Pleasure*, 1972, by David McFadden; for "A Man from France" from *A Man to Marry, A Man to Bury*, 1979, by Susan Musgrave; for "At the Quinte Hotel" and "Home-Made Beer" from *Selected Poems*, 1972, and for "Birdwatching at the Equator" from *The Stone Bird*, 1981, by Al Purdy; for "In Defense of Free Lust" from *Listen to the Old Mother*, 1975, by Helene Rosenthal; for "Bonne Entente," "National Identity," "W.L.M.K.," "Martinigram," and "The Canadian Authors Meet" from *Collected Poems of F. R.*

Scott, 1981; for Life on the *Land Grant Review*" and "Poem Composed..." from *Waiting for Wayman*, 1973, and for "Travelling Companions" from *Living on the Ground*, 1980, by Tom Wayman.

David McFadden for "Journey to Love."

McGraw-Hill Ryerson Limited for "The Poet Is Bidden to Manhattan Island" from *Collected Poems of Sir Charles G. D. Roberts*, 1936, and for "Pullman Porter" from *Collected Poems of Robert Service*, 1907.

Eugene McNamara for "The People Next Door" and "June Allyson" from *Screens*, 1977, Coach House Press.

Florence McNeil for "The Halfmoon Bay Improvement Society."

Susan Musgrave for "My Boots Drive Off in a Cadillac."

Suniti Namjoshi for "Giraffes Are All Right."

John Newlove for "Love Letter" from *Moving In Alone*, 1965 and 1977, Oolichan Books, and for "What Do You Want?" and "Harry, 1967" from *The Fat Man*, 1977, McClelland and Stewart.

bp Nichol for "Billy Pertwilly" and "Wild Bill the Goat."

Alden Nowlan for "First Lessons in Theology" and "Election Song."

Oberon Press for "The Bourgeois Child" and "The Opener" from *The Colour of the Times*, 1964, by Raymond Souster.

Michael Ondaatje for "Postcard from Picadilly Street" and "The Strange Case" from *There's a Trick with a Knife that I'm Learning to Do*, 1979, McClelland and Stewart, and for "The Linguistic War Between Men and Women" from *Canadian Forum*, April 1980.

P. K. Page for "Truce" and "Stefan."

Al Pittmann for "The Artist's Lot" from *Once When I Was Drowning*, 1978, Breakwater Books.

Daniel G. Ray for "Canadiana."

Kevin Roberts for "The Publican's Dog."

Joe Rosenblatt for "How Mice Make Love."

Stephen Scriver for "Once Is Once Too Many."

Richard Sommer for "The Meaning of the Meaning of Poetry."

Francis Sparshott for "Vaughan's World," "Roman Numeral," "Applied Criminology," "Wasp Winter" and "Overheard at a Taxpayer's Meeting."

John Steffler for "My Latest Invention" from *An Explanation of Yellow*, 1981, Borealis Press.

Barry Stevens for "Grade Five Geography Lesson."

Andrew Suknaski for "Koonohple."

Fraser Sutherland for "Celebration."

Sharon Thesen for "After Joe Clark Winning the Federal Election" and "Getting On with It" from *Artemis Hates Romance*, 1980, Coach House Press.

Colleen Thibadeau for "Troubles at Caraquet" and "All My Nephews Have Gone to the Tar Sands."

Thistledown Press for "Weather Lore" from *Blue Sunrise*, 1980, by Bert Almon; for "Capitalism" and "Men, Snoring" from *Land of Peace*, 1980 by Leona Gom; for "Dark Morning" from *Winter You Sleep*, 1980, John V. Hicks; for "The Hustlers" from *Ancestral Dances*, 1979, by Glen Sorestad.

J. O. Thompson for "Fuel Crisis" from *Echo and Montana*, 1980, Longspoon Press.

Polly Thompson for "Me and You."

Turnstone Press for "1949" and "East-North-East" from *Rehearsal for Dancers*, 1978, by Craig Powell; for "The Elephant Dream" from *A Game of Angels*, 1980, by Anne Szumigalski; for "The True Meaning of Being a Man" from *The Earth Is One Body*, 1979, by David Waltner-Toews.

Phyllis Webb for "Alex" from *Selected Poems, 1954-1965*, 1971, Talonbooks; and for "Edmonton Centre."

Jon Whyte for "A Little Black Poem."

The Estate of Anne Wilkinson for "Leda in Stratford, Ont." from *The Collected Poems of Anne Wilkinson*, 1968, Macmillan of Canada.

Christopher Wiseman for "In the Basement."

Elizabeth Woods for "More than a Question of Taste" from *Men*, 1979, Fiddlehead Poetry Books.

Robert Zend for "A Chain of Haik" and "World's Shortest Pessimistic Poem."

Susan Zimmermann for "Love's Humours" from *Nothing Is Lost*, 1980, Caitlin Press.

Index